BY THE SAME WRITER

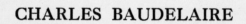

CHARLES BAUDELAIRE

EMILE DE ROY, 1844

CHARLES BAUDELAIRE

A STUDY

BY

ARTHUR SYMONS

NEW YORK
E. P. DUTTON & COMPANY
681 FIFTH AVENUE
MCMXX

TO
JOHN QUINN

CONTENTS

LIST OF ILLUSTRATIONS

BAUDELAIRE: A STUDY

I

WHEN Baudelaire is great, when his genius is
at its highest point of imaginative creation,
of imaginative criticism, it is never when he works by
implication—as the great men who are pure artists
(for instance, Shakespeare) work by implication only
—but always from his personal point of view being
simply infallible and impeccable. The pure artist,
it has been said, never asserts: and the instances
are far from being numerous; Balzac asserts, and
Balzac is always absolutely just in all his assertions:
he whose analysis of modern Society—*La Comédie
Humaine*—verges almost always on creation; and
despite certain deficiencies in technique and in style,
he remains the greatest of all novelists. As for Baudelaire, he rarely asserts; he more often suggests or
divines—with that exquisite desire of perfect and just
work that is always in him. With his keen vision he
rarely misses the essential; with his subtle and
sifted prose he rarely fails in characterizing the right
man in the right way and the wrong man—the man
who is not an artist—in forms of ironical condemnation. Shelley in his time and Blake in his time gave

grave enough offence and perplexity ; so did Baudelaire, so did Poe, so did Swinburne, so did Rossetti,
so did Beardsley. All had their intervals of revolt—
spiritual or unspiritual, according to the particular
trend of their genius ; some destroy mendacious idols,
some change images into symbols ; some are supposed
to be obscurely original. All had to apprehend,
as Browning declared in regard to his readers and
critics in one of his Prefaces, " charges of being wil-
fully obscure, unconscientiously careless, or perversely
harsh." And all these might have said as he said :
" I blame nobody, least of all myself, who did my
best then and since."

In our approach to the poetry, or to the prose, of
any famous writer, with whom we are concerned, we
must necessarily approach his personality ; in appre-
hending it we apprehend him, and certainly we cannot
love it without loving him. As for Baudelaire, I must
confess that, in spite of the fact that one might hate
or love the man according to the judgment of the wise
or of the unwise, I find him more lovable than hateful.
That he failed in trying to love one woman is as
certain as his disillusion after he had possessed her ;
that, in regard to Jeanne Duval, she was to him
simply a silent instrument that, by touching all the
living strings of it, he awakened to a music that is
all his own ; that whether this " masterpiece of flesh "
meant more to him than certain other women who
inspired him in different ways ; whether he thirsted
to drain her " empty kiss " or the " empty kiss " of
Rachel, of Marguerite, of Gabrielle, of Judith, is a
matter of but little significance. A man's life such as

his is a man's own property and the property of no one else. And Baudelaire's conclusion as to any of these might be, perhaps, summed up in this stanza :

" Your sweet, scarce lost estate
    Of innocence, the candour of your eyes,
    Your child-like, pleased surprise,
    Your patience : these afflict me with a weight
    As of some heavy wrong that I must share
    With God who made, with man who found you, fair."

" In more ways than one do men sacrifice to the rebellious angels," says Saint Augustine ; and Beardsley's sacrifice, along with that of all great decadent art, the art of Rops or of Baudelaire, is really a sacrifice to the eternal beauty, and only seemingly to the powers of evil. And here let me say that I have no concern with what neither he nor I could have had absolute knowledge of, his own intention in his work. A man's intention, it must be remembered—and equally in the case of much of the work of Poe and of Baudelaire, much less so in the case of Balzac and Verlaine—from the very fact that it is conscious, is much less intimately himself than the sentiment which his work conveys to me.

Baudelaire's figures, exactly like those designed by Beardsley and by Rodin, have the sensitiveness of the spirit and that bodily sensitiveness which wastes their veins and imprisons them in the attitude of their luxurious meditation. They have nothing that is merely " animal " in their downright course towards repentance ; no overwhelming passion hurries them beyond themselves ; they do not capitulate to an open assault of the enemy of souls. It is the soul in them that sins, sorrowfully, without reluctance, inevitably. Their bodies are eager and faint with wantonness ; they desire fiercer and more exquisite pains, a more intolerable suspense than there is in the world.

Beardsley is the satirist of an age without convictions, and he can but paint hell as Baudelaire did, without pointing for contrast to any actual paradise. He employs the same rhetoric as Baudelaire — a method of emphasis which it is uncritical to think insincere. In the terrible annunciation of evil which he called *The Mysterious Rose-Garden*, the lantern-bearing angel with winged sandals whispers, from among the falling roses, tidings of more than " pleasant sins." And in Baudelaire, as in Beardsley, the peculiar efficacy of their satire is that it is so much the satire of desire returning on itself, the mockery of desire enjoyed, the mockery of desire denied. It is because these love beauty that beauty's degradation obsesses them ; it is because they are supremely conscious of virtue that vice has power to lay hold on them. And with these— unlike other satirists of our day—it is always the soul, and not the body's discontent only, which cries out of these insatiable eyes, that have looked on all their lusts ; and out of these bitter mouths, that have eaten the dust of all their sweetnesses ; and out of these hands, that have laboured delicately for nothing ; and out of their feet, that have run after vanities.

The body, in the arms of death, the soul, in the arms of the naked body : these are the strangest symbolical images of Life and of Death. So, as Flaubert's devotion to art seemed to have had about it something of the " seriousness and passion that are like a consecration," I give this one sentence on the death of Emma Bovary : " Ensuite il recita le *Misereatur* et *l'Indulgentiam,* trempa son pouce droit dans l'huile et commença les onctions : d'abord sur les yeux, qui avaient tant convoité toutes les somptuosites ter-restres ; puis sur les narines, friandes de brises tièdes et de senteurs amoureuses ; puis sur la bouche, qui s'était ouverte pour le mensonge, qui avait gémi d'orgueil et crié dans la luxure ; puis sur les mains, qui se delectaient au contacts suaves, et enfin sur la plante des pieds, si rapides autrefois quand elle courait à l'assouvissance de ses désirs et qui maintenant ne marcheraient plus."

Charles Baudelaire was born April 9th, 1821, in la rue Saint Augustin, 8 ; he was baptized at Saint-Sulpice. His father, François, who had married Mlle Janin in 1803, married, after her death, Caroline Archimbaut-Dufays, born in London, September 27th, 1793. François Baudelaire's father, named Claude, married Marie-Charlotte Dieu, February 10th, 1738, at Neuville-au-Port, in the Department of Marne.

From 1838 to 1842 (when Baudelaire attains his majority) there is a family crisis in a certainly impos-sible family circle. These years he spends in vaga-bonding at his own will : living a deliciously depraved life ; diving, perhaps, into depths of impurity ; haunt-ing the night resorts that one finds in the most curious quarters of Paris—the cafés, the theatres, la Rue de Bréda. He amuses himself enormously : even in " the expense of spirit in a waste of shame ; " he lives then, as always, by his sensitive nerves, by his inexhaustible curiosity. He is devoured then, as always, by the

B

inner fires of his genius and of his sensuality ; and is, certainly, a quite naturally immoral man in his relations with women.

He lives, as I have said; he feeds himself on his nerves :

"The modern malady of love is nerves."

It is an incurable, a world-old malady ; and, from Catullus, one of the greatest of all poets, century after century, from the Latin poets of the Middle Ages, from the poets of the Renaissance, of the Elizabethan Age, down to the modern Romantic Movement, no poet who was a passionate lover of Woman has ever failed to sing for her and against her :

" I hate and I love : you ask me how I can do it ?
I know not : I know that it hurts : I am going through it."

Odi et amo ; quari id faciam, fortasse requiris.
Nescio ; sed fiere sentio, et excrucior.

" Caelius, Lesbia mine, that Lesbia, that
Lesbia whom Catullus for love did rate
Higher than all himself and than all things, stands
Now at the cross-roads and the alleys to wait
For the lords of Rome, with public lips and hands."

Coeli, Lesbia nostra, Lesbia illa,
Illa Lesbia, quam Catullus unam
Plus, quàm se, atque suos amavit omnes.

Need I quote more than these three lines ? These lines, and those quoted above, are enough to show, for all time, that Catullus was as passionate a lover and as passionate a hater of flesh as Villon. Yet, if we are to understand Villon rightly, we must not reject even *le grosse Margot* from her place in his life ; who, to a certainty, had not for one instant the place in his life that Lesbia had in the life of Catullus. Villon was no dabbler in infamy, but one who liked infamous things for their own sake.

Nor must I forget John Donne, whose quality of passion is unique in English poetry—a reasonable rapture, and yet carried to a pitch of actual violence: his senses speak with unparalleled directness; he can exemplify every motion with an unluxurious explicitness which leaves no doubt of his intentions. He suffers from all the fevers and colds of love; and, in his finest poem—a hate poem—he gives expression to a whole region of profound human sentiment which has never been expressed, out of Catullus, with such intolerable truth:

> " When, by thy scorn, O murdress, I am dead,
> And that thou thinkest thee free
> From all solicitations of me,
> Then shall my ghost come to thy bed,
> And thee, feigned vestal, in worse arms shall see:
> Then thy sick taper will begin to wink,
> And he, whose thou art then, being tired before,
> Will, if thou stir, or pinch to wake him, think
> Thou call'st for more,
> And, in false sleep, will from thee shrink;
> And then, poor aspen wretch, neglected thou
> Bathed in a cold, quick-silver sweat will lie
> A verier ghost than I.
> What I will say, I will not tell thee now,
> Lest that preserve thee; and since my love is spent,
> I'd rather thou shouldst painfully repent,
> Than by my threatenings rest still innocent."

As for Baudelaire's adventures when he is sent, perhaps against his will, in May, 1841, on a long voyage from Bordeaux to Calcutta, to return to Paris in February, 1843, after six months' travel, it is conjecturable that he might return a changed man. Certainly his imagination found in the East a curious fascination, with an actual reawakening of new instincts ; and with that oppressive sense of extreme heat, as intense, I suppose, as in Africa, which makes one suffer, bodily and spiritually, and in ways more extraordinary than those who have never endured those tropical heats can possibly conceive of. There he may have abandoned himself to certain obscure rites that to him might have been an initiation into the cults of the Black Venus. And, with these hot suns, these burning midnoons, these animal passions, the very seductiveness of the nakedness of bronze skin, what can I imagine but this : that they lighted in his veins an intolerable flame, that burned there ardently to the end ?

For in his *Wagner* (1861) he writes : " The radiant ancient Venus, Aphrodite, born of white foam, has not imprudently traversed the horrible darkness of the Middle Ages. She has retired to the depths of a cavern, magnificently lighted by the fires that are not those of the Sun. In her descent under earth, Venus has come near to hell's mouth, and she goes, certainly, to many abominable solemnities, to render homage to the Arch-demon, Prince of the Flesh and Lord of Sin." He finds her in the music where Wagner has created a furious song of the flesh, with an absolute knowledge of what in men is diabolical. " For from the first measures, the nerves vibrate in unison with the melody ; one's flesh remembers itself and begins to tremble. *Tannhäuser* represents the eternal combat between the two principles that have chosen the human heart as battle-field, that is to say, of the flesh with the spirit, of hell with heaven, of Satan with God."

In January, 1843, Baudelaire finds himself in possession of a fortune of seventy-five thousand francs. With his incurable restlessness, his incurable desire of change, he is always moving from one place to another. He takes rooms at Quai de Bethune, 10, Isle-Saint-Louis ; rue Vanneau, faubourg Saint-Germain ; rue Varenne, quai d'Anjou ; Hôtel Pimodan, 17 ; Hôtel Corneille ; Hôtel Folkestone, rue Lafitte ; Avenue de la République, 95 ; rue des Marais-du-Temple, 25 ; rue Mazarine ; rue de Babylone ; rue de Seine, 57 ; rue Pigalle, 60 ; Hôtel Voltaire, 19 quai Voltaire ; rue Beautrellis, 22 ; Cité d'Orléans, 15 ; rue d'Angoulême-du-Temple, 18 ; Hôtel Dieppe, rue d'Amsterdam, 22 ; rue des Ecuries-d'Artois, 6 ; rue de Seine, l'Hôtel du Maroc, 35.

With a certain instinct for drawing Baudelaire haunts many painter's studios : Delacroix's, whose genius he discovers, giving him much of his fame, becoming his intimate friend ; Manet's, whose genius he also divines and discovers ; Daumier's, to whom he attributes " the strange and astonishing qualities of a great genius, sick of genius." So also, from the beginning, Baudelaire's judgments are infallibly right ; so also his first book, *Le Salon de* 1845, has all the insolence of youth and all the certitude of a youth of genius. But his fame is made, that is to say, as an imaginative critic, with *Le Salon de* 1846 ; for, after the prelude, the entire book is fascinating, paradoxical,

and essentially æsthetical ; a wonderful book in which
he reveals the mysteries of colour, of form, of design,
of technique, and of the enigmas of creative works.
Here he elaborates certain of his mature theories, such
as his exultant praise—in which he is one with Lamb
and with Swinburne ; his just disdain, and his grave
irony, in which he is one with Swinburne ; and, above
all, that passionate love of all forms of beauty, at once
spiritual and absolute, which is part of the quintes-
sence of his genius.

So, as Swinburne, in the fire of his youthful genius,
was the first to praise Baudelaire in English, I quote
these sentences of his from an essay on Tennyson and
Musset : " I do not mean that the *Comédie de le Mort*
must be ranked with the *Imitation of Christ*, or that
Les Fleurs du Mal should be bound up with *The Christian Year*. But I do say that no principle of art which
does not exclude from its tolerance the masterpieces
of Titian can logically or consistently reject the masterpieces of a poet who has paid to one of them the most
costly tribute of carven verse, in lines of chiselled ivory
with rhymes of ringing gold, that ever was laid by the
high priest of one muse on the high altar of another.
And I must also maintain my opinion that the per-
vading note of spiritual tragedy in the brooding verse
of Baudelaire dignifies and justifies at all points his
treatment of his darkest and strangest subjects. The
atmosphere of his work is to the atmosphere of
Gautier's as the air of a gas-lit alcove is to the air of
the far-flowering meadows that make in April a natural
Field of the Cloth of Gold all round the happier poet's
native town of Tarbes, radiant as the open scroll of

his writings with immeasurable wealth of youth and
sunlight and imperishable spring. The sombre star-
light under which Baudelaire nursed and cherished the
strange melancholy of his tropical home-sickness, with
its lurid pageant of gorgeous or of ghastly dreams, was
perhaps equidistant from either of these, but assuredly
had less in common with the lamplight than the sun-
shine."

To roam in the sun and air with vagabonds, as
Villon and his infamous friends did on their wonderful
winter nights, " where the wolves live on wind," and
where the gallows stands at street corners, ominously,
and one sees swing in the wind dead chained men ; to
haunt the strange streets of cities, to know all the
useless and improper and amusing, the moral and the
immoral people, who are alone worth knowing ; to
live, as well as to observe ; to be drawn out of the
rapid current of life into an exasperating inaction : it
is such things as these that make for poetry and for
prose. Some make verse out of personal sensations,
verse which is half pathological, which is half physio-
logical ; some out of colours and scents and crowds
and ballets ; some out of music, out of the sea's
passions ; some simply out of rhythms that insist on
being used ; a few out of the appreciation of the
human comedy. The outcome of many experiments,
these must pass beyond that stage into the stage of
existence.

So, in much of Baudelaire's verse I find not only the
exotic (rarely the erotic) but, in the peculiar technique
of the lines, certain andante movements, lingering
subtleties of sound, colour, and suggestion, with—at

times, but never in the excessive sense of Flaubert's—the almost medical curiosity of certain researches into the stuff of dreams, the very fibre of life itself, which, combined, certainly tend to produce a new thing in poetry. A new order of phenomena absorbs his attention, which becomes more and more externalized, more exclusively concerned with the phenomena of the soul, with morbid sensation, with the curiosities of the mind and the senses. Humanity is now apprehended in a more than ever generalized and yet specialized way in its essence, when it becomes, if you will, an abstraction ; or, if you will, for the first time purely individual.

In certain poets these have been foiled endeavours ; in Baudelaire never : for one must never go beyond the unrealizable, never lose one's intensity of expression, never let go of the central threads of one's spider's web. Still, in regard to certain direct pathological qualities, there is a good deal of this to be found in much of the best poetry—in Poe, in Rossetti, in Swinburne's earlier work, and much in Baudelaire ; only all these are moved by a fascination : in Poe for the fantastically inhuman ; in Rossetti for the inner life of the imagination, for to him, as Pater said, " life is a crisis at every moment ; " in Swinburne for the arduous fulness of intricate harmony, and for the essentially lyric quality, joy, in almost unparalleled abundance.

There can hardly be a poet who is not conscious of how little his own highest powers are under his own control. The creation of beauty is the end of art, but the artist—whether he be Baudelaire or Verlaine—

should rarely admit to himself that such is his purpose. A poem is not written by a man who says : I will sit down and write a poem ; but rather by the man who, captured by rather than capturing on impulse, hears a tune which he does not recognize, or sees a sight which he does not remember, in some " close corner of his brain," and exerts the only energy at his disposal in recording it faithfully, in the medium of his particular art. And so in every creation of beauty, some obscure desire stirred in the soul, not realized by the mind for what it was, and, aiming at much more minor things in the world than pure beauty, produced it. Now, to the critic this is not more important to remember than it is for him to remember that the result, the end, must be judged, not by the impulse which brought it into being, nor by the purpose which it sought to serve, but by the success or failure in one thing : the creation of beauty. To the artist himself this precise consciousness of what he has done is not always given, any more than a precise consciousness of what he is doing.

To Baudelaire as to Pater there were certain severe tests of the effects made on us by works of genius. In both writers there is a finality of creative criticism. For, to these, all works of art, all forms of human life, were as powers and forces producing pleasurable sensations. One can find them in a gem, a wine, a spoken word, a sudden gesture, in anything, indeed, that strikes vividly or fundamentally the senses, that acts instantaneously on one's perceptive passions. "What," says Pater in his essay on Wordsworth, " are the peculiarities in things and persons which he values, the impression and sense of which he can convey to others, in an extraordinary way ? "

" The ultimate aim of criticism," said Coleridge, " is much more to establish the principles of writing than to furnish rules how to pass judgment on what has been written by others." And for this task he had an incomparable foundation : imagination, insight, logic, learning, almost every critical quality united in one ; and he was a poet who allowed himself to be a critic. Certainly, Baudelaire shared certain of those qualities ; indeed, almost all ; even, in a sense, logic. His genius was so great, and in its greatness so many-sided, that for some studious disciples of the rarer kind he will doubtless, seen from any possible point of view, have always some of his magic and of his magnetism. The ardour, delicacy, energy of his intellect, his resolute desire to get at the root of things and deeper yet, if deeper might be, will always enchant and attract all spirits of like mould and temper ; that is to say, those that are most morbid, most fond of imaginative per-versities.

Prose, I have said, listens at the doors of all the senses, and repeats their speech almost in their own terms. But poetry (it is Baudelaire who says it) " is akin to music through a prosody whose roots plunge deeper in the human soul than any classical theory has defined." Poetry begins where prose ends, and it is at its chief peril that it begins sooner. The one safe-guard for the poet is to say to himself : What I can write in prose I will not allow myself to write in verse, out of mere honour towards my material. The farther I can extend my prose, the farther back do I set the limits of verse. The region of poetry will thus be always the beyond, the ultimate, and with the least possible chance of any confusion of territory.

Prose is the language of what we call real life, and it is only in prose that an illusion of external reality can be given. Compare, not only the surroundings, the sense of time, and locality, but the whole process and existence of character, in a play of Shakespeare and in a novel of Balzac. I choose Balzac among novelists because his mind is nearer to what is creative in the poet's mind than that of any novelist, and his method nearer to the method of the poets. Take *King Lear* and take *Père Goriot*. Goriot is a Lear at heart ; and he suffers the same tortures and humiliations. But precisely when Lear grows up before the mind's eye into a vast cloud and shadowy monument of trouble, Goriot grows downward into the earth and takes root there, wrapping the dust about all his fibres. It is part of his novelty that he comes so close to us and is so recognizable. Lear may exchange his crown for a fool's bauble, knowing nothing of it ; but Goriot knows well enough the value of every bank-note that his daughter robs him of. In that definiteness, that new power of " stationary " emotion in a firm and material way, lies one of the great opportunities of prose.

So it is Baudelaire who has said this fundamental thing on the problem of artist and critic : " It would be a wholly new event in the history of the arts if a critic were to turn himself into a poet, a reversal of every psychic law, a monstrosity ; on the other hand, all great poets become naturally, inevitably, critics.

I pity the critics who are guided solely by instinct ; they seem to me incomplete. In the spiritual life of the former there must be a crisis when they would think out their art, discover the obscure laws in consequence of which they have produced, and draw from this study a series of precepts whose divine purpose is infallibility in poetic construction. It would be prodigious for a critic to become a poet, and it is impossible for a poet not to contain a critic."

Dessin de Charles Baudelaire fait chez moi le 2 novembre 1860.

E. G.

HAS any writer ever explained the exact meaning of the word Style ? To me nothing is more difficult. Technique, that is quite a different affair. The essence of good style might be, as Pater says, "expressiveness," as, for instance, in Pascal's style, which—apart from that—is the purest style of any French writer. It is no paradox to state this fact : without technique, perfect of its kind, no one is worth considering in any art ; the violinist, the pianist, the painter, the poet, the novelist, the rope-dancer, the acrobat—all, without exception, if they lapse from technique lapse from perfection. I have often taken Ysaye as the type of the artist, not because he is faultless in technique, but because he begins to create his art at the point where faultless technique leaves off.

Art, said Aristotle, should always have "a continual slight novelty," and his meaning is that art should never astonish. Take, for instance, Balzac, Villiers, Poe, and Baudelaire ; only one part of their genius, but a most sinister one, is the desire to astonish. There is, to me, nothing more astonishing in prose fiction than *The Pit and the Pendulum* and *The Cask of Amontillado* of Poe ; they are more than analysis, though this is pushed to the highest point of analysis ; they have in them a slow, poisonous and cruel logic ; equalled only, and at times surpassed in their imagination, by certain of Villiers' *Contes Cruels*, such as his *Demoiselles de Bien Filâtre, L'Intersigne* and *Les Amants de Tolède*. And—what is more astonishing in his prose than in any of the writers I have mentioned —is his satire ; a satire which is the revenge of beauty on ugliness ; and therefore the only laughter of our time which is fundamental, as fundamental as that of Rabelais and of Swift.

Baudelaire, when he astonishes, is never satirical : sardonical, ironical, coldly cruel, irritating, and persistent. This form of astonishment is an inveterate part of the man's sensitive and susceptible nature. It is concentrated, inimical, a kind of juggling or fencing ; a form of contradiction, of mystification ; and a deliberate desire of causing bewilderment. The Philistine can never pardon a mystification, and a fantastic genius—such as that of Baudelaire and of Poe—can never resist it when opportunity offers.

Had he but been one of those " elect souls, vessels of election, *épris des hauteurs,* as we see them pass across the world's stage, as if led on by a kind of thirst for God ! " (I quote Pater's words on Pascal) his sombre soul might have attained an ultimate peace ; a peace beyond all understanding. This was cruelly denied him. He, I imagine, believed in God ; thirsted for God : neither was his belief confirmed nor his thirst assuaged. He might, for all I know, have thought himself a reprobate—and so cast out of God's sight.

> " For, till the thunder in the trumpet be,
> Soul may divide from body, but not we
> One from another ; I hold thee with my hand,
> I let mine eyes have all their will of thee,

> I seal myself upon thee with my might,
> Abiding alway out of all men's sight
> Until God loosen over sea and land
> The thunder of the trumpets of the night."

I am certain Baudelaire must have read the poems of John Keats ; for there are certain characteristics in the versification and in the using of images of both poets. Keats had something feminine and twisted in his mind, made up out of unhealthy nerves—which are utterly lacking in Baudelaire—but which it is now the fashion to call decadent ; Keats being more than a decadent, but certainly decadent in such a line as—

> " One faint eternal eventide of gems,"

which might have been written, in jewelled French, by Mallarmè. I give one of his sonnets, a perverse and perverted one, made by a fine technical feat out of two recurrent rhymes :

> " Ses purs ongles très-haut dédiant leur onyx,
> L'angoisse, ce minuit, soutient, lampadaphore,
> Maint rêve vesperal brûlé par le Phénix
> Que ne recueille pas de cinéraire amphore
>
> Sur les crédences, au salon vide : nul ptyx
> Aboli bibelot d'inanité sonore,
> (Car le maître est allé puiser des fleurs au Styx
> Avec ce seul objet dont le néant s'honore.)
>
> Mais proche la croisée au nord vacante, un or
> Agonise selon peut-être le décor
> Des licornes ruant du feu contre une nixe,
>
> Elle, défunte nue en le miroir, encor
> Que, dans l'oubli formé par le cadre, se fixe
> De scintillations sitôt le septuor."

Keats luxuriates, like Baudelaire, in the details of physical discomfort, in all their grotesque horror, as when, in sleeplessness—how often these two over-strung and over-nervous poets must have had sleepless nights !—

> " We put our eyes into a pillowy cleft,
> And see the spangly gloom froth up and boil."

He is neo-Latin, again like Baudelaire, in his insistence on the physical sensations of his lovers, the bodily translations of emotion. In Venus, leaning over Adonis, he notes :

> " When her lips and eyes
> Were closed in sullen moisture, and quick sighs
> Came vexed and panting through her nostrils small."

And, in another line, he writes :

> " By the moist languor of thy breathing face."

Lycius, in *Lamia :*

> " Sick to lose
> The amorous promise of her lone complain,
> Swooned murmuring of love, and pale with pain ; "

and all that trembling and swooning of his lovers, which English critics have found unmanly, would at all events be very much at home in modern French poetry, where love is again, as it was to Catullus and Propertius, a sickness, an entrancing madness, a poisoning. To find anything like it, like this utter subtlety of expression, we must go back to the Elizabethan Age, and then look forward, and find, beyond Keats, traces of it in Rossetti and in Morris's *The Defence of Guinevere ;* as, for instance, in some of the Queen's lines :

COINS

génois — genoa
florin — florence
ducat
zecchino } venice

Oxford 1167
Cambridge 1209?

"Listen, suppose your turn were come to die,
And you were quite alone and very weak ;
Yea, laid a dying while very mightily

The wind was ruffling up the narrow streak
Of river through your broad lands running well ;
Suppose a hush should come, then some one speak :

One of these cloths is heaven, and one is hell,
Now choose one cloth for ever, which they be,
I shall not tell you, you must somehow tell

Of your own strengths and mightiness ; here, see ! '
Yea, yea, my lord, and you to ope your eyes,
At foot of your familiar bed to see

A great God's angel standing, with such dyes,
Not known on earth, on his great wings, and hands,
Hold out two ways, light from the inner skies

Showing him well, and making his commands
Seem to be God's commands, moreover, too,
Holding within his hands the cloths on wands ;

And one of these strange choosing cloths was blue,
Wavy and long, and one cut short and red :
No man could tell the better of the two.

After a shivering half-hour you said :
'God help ! Heaven's colour, the blue'; and he said, 'Hell !'
Perhaps you then would roll upon your bed,

And cry to all good men that loved you well,
' Ah, Christ ! If only I had known, known, known ; '
Launcelot went away, then I could tell,

Like wisest men, how all things would be, moan,
And roll and hurt myself, and long to die,
And yet fear much to die for what was sown.

Nevertheless you, O Sir Gawaine, lie,
Whatever may have happened through these years,
God knows I speak truth, saying that you lie."

All these rough, harsh *terza-rime* lines are wonderful enough in their nakedness of sensations—sensations of heat, of hell, of heaven, of colours, of death, of life, of moans, and of lies. It is, in a sense, as far as such experiments go, a return to the Middle Ages ; to what was exotic in them and strange and narcotic. Only here, as in *Les Litanies de Satan* of Baudelaire—to which they have some remote likeness—there are no interludes of wholesome air, as through open doors, on these hot, impassioned scenes.

Rossetti says somewhere that no modern poet, and that few poets of any century, ever compressed into so small a space so much imaginative material as he himself always did ; and this, I conceive, partly, also, from that almost child-like imagination of his, for all its intellectual subtlety, that dominated him to such an extent that to tell him anything of a specially tragic or pathetic nature was cruel, so vividly did he realize every situation ; and also because of his wonderful saying in regard to his own way of weaving an abominable line at the end of one of his finest sonnets into a sublime one :

" Life touching lips with Immortality : "

that the line he had used before belonged to the class of phrase absolutely forbidden in poetry. " It is intellectually incestuous poetry seeking to beget its emotional offspring on its own identity ; whereas the present line gives only the momentary contact with the immortal which results from sensuous culmination, and is always a half-conscious element of it."

Now, to me, both Keats before him and Baudelaire

in his own generation, had the same excessive sense of
concentration. " To load every rift with ore : " that,
to Keats, was the essential thing ; and it meant to
pack the verse with poetry so that every line should
be heavy with the stuff of the imagination : the phrase
I have given being a rebuke to Shelley, significant of
the art of both poets. For as Keats, almost in the
same degree as Baudelaire, worked on every inch of
his surface, so perhaps no poets ever put so much
poetic detail into so small a space, with, as I have said,
the exception of Rossetti. And, as a matter of fact,
when we examine the question with scrupulous care,
it must be said that both Baudelaire and Keats are
often metrically slipshod.

One of Wagner's ideas, in regard to the artistic
faculty was, receptivity ; the impulse to impart only
what comes when these impressions fill the mind " to an
ecstatic excess ; " and the two forms of the artist : the
feminine, who recoils from life, and the masculine, who
absorbs life. From this follows, in the case of creative
artists such as Baudelaire, the necessity to convey to
others as vividly and intelligibly, as far as possible, what
his own mind's eye had seen. Then one has to seize
everything from which one can wring its secret—its
secret for us and for no one else. And all this, and in
fact the whole of our existence, is partly the conflict
within us of the man with the woman, the male and
the female energies that strive always :

> " Here nature is, alive and untamed,
> Unafraid and unashamed ;
> Here man knows woman with the greed
> Of Adam's wonder, the primal need."

And, in these fundamental lines of Blake :

> " What is it men in women do require ?
> The lineaments of gratified Desire.
> What is it women do in men require ?
> The lineaments of gratified Desire."

And, again, in these more primeval and more essentially animal lines of Rossetti :

> " O my love, O Love—snake of Eden !
> (*And O the bower and the hour !*)
> O to-day and the day to come after !
> Loose me, love—give way to my laughter !
>
> Lo ! two babes for Eve and for Adam !
> (*And O the bower and the hour !*)
> Lo, sweet snake, the travail and treasure—
> Two men-children born for their pleasure !
>
> The first is Cain and the second Abel :
> (*Eden bower's in flower*)
> The soul of one shall be made thy brother,
> And thy tongue shall lap the blood of the other.
> (*And O the bower and the hour !*)."

Baudelaire, in *De l'Essence de Rire*, wrote : " The Romantic School, or, one might say in preference, the Satanical School, has certainly understood the primordial law of laughter. All the melodramatic villains, all those who are cursed, damned, fatally marked with a rictus of the lips that extends to the ears, are in the pure orthodoxy of laughter. For the rest, they are for the most part illegitimate sons of the famous Melmoth the Wanderer, the great Satanic creation of Maturin. What can one conceive of as greater, as more powerful, in regard to our humanity than this pale and bored Melmoth ? He is a living contradiction ; that is why his frozen laughter freezes and wrenches the entrails."

Distinctly the most remarkable of the British triumvirate which in the early part of the century won a momentary fame as the school of horror, Maturin is much less known to the readers of to-day than either Monk Lewis or Mrs. Radcliffe. Thanks to Balzac, who did *Melmoth* the honour of a loan in *Melmoth Reconcilié*, Maturin has attained a certain fame in France—which, indeed, he still retains. *Melmoth* has to-day in France something of that reputation which has kept alive another English book, *Vathek*. Did not Balzac, in a moment of indiscriminating enthusiasm, couple the *Melmoth* of Maturin with the *Don Juan* of Molière, the *Faust* of Goethe, the *Manfred* of Byron—*grandes images tracées par les plus grands génies de l'Europe ?* In other words, Maturin had his day of fame, in which even men like Scott and Byron were led into a sympathetic exaggeration. There's one exception. That Coleridge was hostile, possibly unjust, is likely enough. It should be mentioned that in 1816 the Drury Lane Committee, who had, reasonably enough, rejected a play by Coleridge, accepted a monstrous production of Maturin's named *Bertram*. The *gros bon mélodrame*, as Balzac calls it, was a great success. " It is all sound and fury, signifying nothing," said Kean, who acted in it ; and Kean, who knew his public, realized that that was why it succeeded. The play was printed, and ran through seven editions, sinking finally to the condition of a chap-book, in which its horrors were to be had for sixpence. On this pretentious work Coleridge—for what reasons we need not inquire—took the trouble to write an article, or, as it was phrased, to make an attack. To this Maturin wrote a violent reply, which the good advice of Scott prevented him from publishing. It is curious at the present day to read the letter in which Scott urges upon Maturin the wisdom of silence—not because he is likely to get the worst of the battle, but, among other reasons, because " Coleridge's work has been little read or heard of, and has made no general impression whatever—certainly no impression unfavourable to you or your play. In the opinion of many, therefore, you will be resenting an injury of which they are unacquainted with the existence."

The episode is both comic and instructive. Coleridge and Maturin ! Scott urging on Maturin the charity of mercy to Coleridge, as---" Coleridge has had some room to be spited at the world, and you are, I trust, to continue to be a favourite with the public ! " Poor Maturin, far from continuing to be a favourite with the public, outlived his reputation in the course of a somewhat short life. He died at the age of forty-three. Like the hero of Baudelaire's whimsical and delicious little tale *La Fanfarlo*, he preferred artifice to nature, especially when it was unnecessary. Such is the significant gossip which we have about the personality of Maturin—gossip which brings out clearly the deliberate eccentricity which marks his work, which one sees also in the foppish affected and lackadaisical creature who looks at the reader as if he were admiring himself before his mirror.

The word " genius," indeed, is too lofty an epithet to use regarding a man of great talent certainly, but of nothing more than erratic and melodramatic talent. *Melmoth the Wanderer* is in parts very thrilling ; its Elizabethan feast of horrors has a savour as of a lesser Tourneur. But it is interesting only in parts, and at its best it never comes near the effect which the great masters of the grotesque and terrible—Hoffmann, Poe, Villiers de l'Isle-Adam—have known how to produce. A freak of construction, which no artist could have been guilty of, sends us wandering from story to story in a very maze of underplots and episodes and inter-polations. Six separate stories are told—all in paren-thesis—and the greater part of the book is contained within inverted commas. What is fine in it is the vivid, feverish way in which, from time to time, some story of horror or mystery is forced home to one's sensations. It is the art of the nightmare, and it has none of the supremacy in that line of the *Contes Drôla-tiques* of Balzac. But certain scenes in the monastery and in the prisons of the Inquisition—an attempted escape, a scene where an immured wretch fights the reptiles in the darkness—are full of a certain kind of power. That escape, for instance, with its conse-quences, is decidedly gruesome, decidedly exciting ; but compare it with Dumas, with the escape of Monte Cristo ; compare it with the yet finer narrative of Casanova—the unsurpassed model of all such narra-tives in fiction. Where Casanova and Dumas produce their effect by a simple statement—a record of external events from which one realizes, as one could realize in no other way, all the emotions and sensations of the persons who were undergoing such experiences— Maturin seeks his effect, and produces it, but in a much

lesser degree, by a sort of excited psychology, an ex-
clamatory insistence on sensation and emotion.
Melmoth the Wanderer is only the object of our his-
torical curiosity. We have, indeed, and shall always
have, " lovers of dark romance."

III

I

BAUDELAIRE'S genius is satanical; he has in a
sense the vision of Satan. He sees in the past
the lusts of the Borgias, the sins and vices of the
Renaissance; the rare virtues that flourish like
flowers and weeds, in brothels and in garrets. He sees
the vanity of the world with finer modern tastes than
Solomon; for his imagination is abnormal, and
divinely normal. In this age of infamous shames he
has no shame. His flesh endures, his intellect is flawless. He chooses his own pleasures delicately, sensi-
tively, as he gathers his exotic *Fleurs du Mal,* in itself
a world, neither a *Divina Commedia* nor *Une Comédie
Humaine,* but a world of his own fashioning.

His vividly imaginative passion, with his instincts
of inspiration, are aided by a determined will, a self-
reserve, an intensity of conception, an implacable insolence, an accurate sense of the exact value of every
word. In the Biblical sense he might have said of his
own verse: " It is bone of my bone, and flesh of my
flesh." The work, as the man, is subtle, strange,
complex, morbid, enigmatical, refined, paradoxical,
spiritual, animal. To him a scent means more than a
sunset, a perfume more than a flower, the tempting
demons more than the unseductive angels. He loves

BAUDELAIRE, DESIGNED BY HIMSELF, 1848

luxury as he loves wine ; a picture of Manet's as a woman's fan.

Fascinated by sin, he is never the dupe of his emotions ; he sees sin as the Original Sin ; he studies sin as he studies evil, with a stern logic ; he finds in horror a kind of attractiveness, as Poe had found it ; rarely in hideous things, save when his sense of what I call a moralist makes him moralize, as in his terrible poem, *Une Charogne.* He has pity for misery, hate for progress. He is analytic, he is a learned casuist, whom I can compare with the formidable Spanish Jesuit, Thomas Sanchez, who wrote the Latin *Aphorismi Matrimonio* (1629).

His soul swims on music played on no human instrument, but on strings that the Devil pulls, to which certain living puppets dance in grotesque fashion, to unheard-of rhythms, to the sound of violins strummed on by evil spirits in Witches' Sabbats. Some swing in the air, as hanged dead people on gallows, and, as their bones rattle in the wind, one sees Judas Iscariot, risen out of Hell for an instant's gratification, as he grimaces on these grimacing visages.

Les Fleurs du Mal is the most curious, subtle, fascinating, and extraordinary creation of an entire world ever fashioned in modern ages. Baudelaire paints vice and degradation of the utmost depth, with cynicism and with pity, as in the poem I have referred to, where the cult of the corpse is the sensuality of ascetism, or the ascetism of sensuality : the mania of fakirs ; material by passion, Christian by perversity.

And, in a sense, he is our modern Catullus ; in his furies, his negations, his outcries, his Paganism, his inconceivable passion for woman's flesh ; yet Lesbia is for ever Lesbia. Still, Baudelaire in his *Franciscae meae Laudes,* and with less sting but with as much sensual sense of the splendour of sex, gives a magnificent Latin eulogy of a learned and pious modiste, that ends :

> " Patera gemmis corusca,
> Panis salsus, mollis esca,
> Divinum vinum, Francisca."

And he praises the Decadent Latin language in these words : "Dans cette merveilleuse langue, le solécisme et le barbarisme me paraissent rendre les négligences forcés d'une passion qui s'oublie et se moque des règles."

Don Juan aux Enfers is a perfect Delacroix. In *Danse Macabre* there is the universal swing of the dancers who dance the Dance of Death. Death herself, in her extreme horror, ghastly, perfumed with myrrh, mixes her irony with men's insanity as she dances the Sabbat of Pleasure. He shows us the infamous menagerie of the vices in the guise of reptiles ; our chief enemy Ennui is *ce monstre délicat.* There are Vampires, agonies of the damned alive ; *Le Possédé* with his excruciating cry out of all his fibres : *O mon cher Belzébuth ! je t'adore !* And there are some, subtler and silent, that seem to move, softly, as the feet of Night, to the sound of faint music, or under the shroud of a sunset.

Les Fleurs du Mal are grown in Parisian soil, exotics that have the strange, secretive, haunting touch and taint of the earth's or of the body's corruption. In his sense of beauty there is a certain revolt, a spiritual malady, which may bring with it the heated air of an

alcove or the intoxicating atmosphere of the East.
Never since Villon has the flesh of woman been more
adored and abhorred. Both aware of the original sin
of *l'unique animal*—the seed of our moral degradation
—Villon creates his *Grosse Margot* and Baudelaire
Delphine et Hippolyte. Villon's is a scullion-wench,
and in the Ballad a Brothel as infamous, as foul, as
abominable as a Roman Lupanar surges before one's
astonished vision. And this comes after his supreme,
his consummate praise of ruinous old age on a harlot's
body : *Les Regrets de la Belle Heaulmière.* It is one
of the immortal things that exist in the world, that I
can compare only with Rodin's statue in bronze : both
equal incarnations of the symbolical conception that
sin brought shame into the first woman's flesh.

" Que m'en reste-il ? Honte et Péché : "

cries each mouth, cries to the end of earth's eternity.

In Baudelaire's *Femmes Damnées* there is the aching
soul of the spirit's fatal malady : that sexual malady
for which there is no remedy : the Lesbian sterile
perilous divinisation of flesh for flesh, virginal or un-
virginal flesh *with* flesh. In vain desire, of that one
desire that exists beyond all possible satisfaction, the
desire of an utter annihilation of body with body in
that ecstasy which can never be absolutely achieved
without man's flesh, they strive, unconsumed with
even the pangs of their fruitless desires. They live
only with a life of desire, and that obsession has carried
them beyond the wholesome bounds of nature into the
violence of a perversity which is at times almost insane.
And all this sorrowful and tortured flesh is consumed

with that feverish desire that leaves them only a short space for their desire's fruitions.

II

Certain of these Flowers of Evil are poisonous ; some are grown in the hotbeds of Hell ; some have the perfume of a serpentine girl's skin ; some the odour of woman's flesh. Certain spirits are intoxicated by these accursed flowers, to save themselves from the too much horror of their vices, from the worse torture of their violated virtues. And a cruel imagination has fashioned these naked images of the Seven Deadly Sins, eternally regretful of their first fall ; that smile not even in Hell, in whose flames they writhe. One conceives them there and between the sun and the earth ; in the air, carried by the winds ; aware of their infernal inheritance. They surge like demons out of the Middle Ages ; they are incapable of imagining God's justice.

Baudelaire dramatizes these living images of his spirit and of his imagination, these fabulous creatures of his inspiration, these macabre ghosts, in a fashion utterly different from that of other tragedians—Shakespeare, and Aristophanes in his satirical Tragedies, his lyrical Comedies ; yet in the same sense of being the writer where beauty marries unvirginally the sons of ancient Chaos.

In these pages swarm (in his words) all the corruptions and all the scepticisms ; ignoble criminals without convictions, detestable hags that gamble, the cats that are like men's mistresses ; Harpagon ; the exquisite, barbarous, divine, implacable, mysterious Madonna of the Spanish style ; the old men ; the

LES
·FLEURS DU MAL

PAR

CHARLES BAUDELAIRE

On dit qu'il faut couler les execrables choses
Dans le puits de l'oubli et au sepulchre encloses,
Et que par les esprits le mal ressuscité
Infectera les mœurs de la postérité ;
Mais le vice n'a point pour mère la science,
Et la vertu n'est pas fille de l'ignorance.

THÉODORE AGRIPPA D'AUBIGNÉ.
(*les Tragiques*, Liv. II).

PARIS

POULET-MALASSIS ET DE BROISE

LIBRAIRES-ÉDITEURS

4, rue de Buci

—

1857

drunkards, the assassins, the lovers (their deaths and
lives) ; the owls ; the vampires whose kisses raise
from the grave the corpse of its own self ; the Irremediable that assails its origin : Conscience in Evil !
There is an almost Christ-like poem on his Passion,
Le Reniement de Saint-Pierre, an almost Satanic de-
nunciation of God in *Abel and Cain,* and with them
the Evil Monk, an enigmatical symbol of Baudelaire's
soul, of his work, of all that his eyes love and hate.
Certain of these creatures play in travesties, dance in
ballets. For all the Arts are transformed, transfigured,
transplanted out of their natural forms to pass in
magnificent state across the stage : the stage with the
abyss of Hell in front of it.

" Sensualist " (I quote a critic), " but the most profound of sensualists, and, furious of being no more
than that, he goes, in his sensation, to the extreme
limit, to the mysterious gate of infinity against which
he knocks, yet knows not how to open, with rage he
contracts his tongue in the vain effort." Yet centuries
before him Dante entered Hell, traversed it in imagination from its endless beginning to its endless end ; returned to earth to write, for the spirit of Beatrice and
for the world, that *Divina Commedia,* of which in
Verona certain women said :

> " Lo, he that strolls to Hell and back
>   At will ! Behold him, how Hell's reek
>   Has crisped his beard and singed his cheek."

It is Baudelaire who, in Hell as in earth, finds a
certain Satan in such modern hearts as his ; that even
modern art has an essentially demoniacal tendency ;

that the infernal pact of man increases daily, as if the
Devil whispered in his ear certain sardonic secrets.
Here in such satanic and romantic atmosphere one
hears dissonances, the discords of the instruments in
the Sabbats, the howlings of irony, the vengeance of
the vanquished.

I give one sentence of Gautier's on Baudelaire.
" This poet of *Les Fleurs du Mal* loved what one
wrongly calls the style of decadence, which is no other
thing than the arrival of art at this extreme point of
maturity that determined in their oblique suns the
civilizations that aged : a style ingenious, complicated,
learned, full of shades and of rarities, turning for ever
backward the limits of the language, using technical
vocabularies, taking colours from all the palettes, notes
from all the keyboards, striving to render one's thought
in what is most ineffable, and form in its most vague
and evasive contours, listening so as to translate them,
the subtle confidences of neurosis, the passionate confessions of ancient passions in their depravity and the
bizarre hallucinations of the fixed idea." He adds :
" In regard to his verse there is the language already
veined in the greenness of decomposition, the tainted
language of the later Roman Empire, and the complicated refinements of the Byzantine School, the last
form of Greek art fallen in delinquencies." See how
perfectly the phrase *la langue de faisandée* suits the
exotic style of Baudelaire !

Yet, tainted as the style is from time to time, never
was the man himself tainted : he who in modern verse
gave first of all an unknown taste to sensations ; he
who painted vice in all its shame ; whose most savor-

ous verses are perfumed as with subtle aromas ; whose
women are bestial, rouged, sterile, bodies without
souls ; whose *Litanies de Satan* have that cold irony
which he alone possessed in its extremity, in these so-
called impious lines which reveal, under whatever
disguise, his belief in a mathematical superiority estab-
lished by God from all eternity, and whose least in-
fraction is punished by certain chastisements, in this
world as in the next.

I can imagine Baudelaire in his hours of nocturnal
terrors, sleepless in a hired woman's bed, saying to
himself these words of Marlowe's *Satan :*

"Why, this is Hell, nor can I out of it !"

in accents of eternal despair wrenched from the lips
of the Arch Fiend. And the genius of Baudelaire, I
can but think, was as much haunted as Marlowe's with,
in Lamb's words, " a wandering in fields where curiosity is forbidden to go, approaching the dark gulf near
enough to look in."

III

Has Baudelaire *l'amour du mal pour le mal ?* In a
certain sense, yes ; in a certain sense, no. He believes
in evil as in Satan and God—the primitive forces that
govern worlds : the eternal enemies. He sees the
germs of evil everywhere, few of the seeds of virtue.
He sees pass before him the world's drama : he is one
of the actors, he plays his parts cynically, ironically.
He speaks in rhythmic cadences.

But, above all, he watches the dancers ; these also
are elemental ; and the tragic fact is that the dancers

D

dance for their living. For their living, for their pleasure, for the pleasure of pleasing others. So passes the
fantastic part of their existence, from the savage who
dances silent dances—for, indeed, all dancers are silent
—but without music, to the dancer who dances for us
on the stage, who turns always to the sound of music.
There is an equal magic in the dance and in song ; both
have their varied rhythms ; both, to use an image, the
rhythmic beating of our hearts. It is imagined that
dancing and music were the oldest of the arts. Rhythm
has rightly been called the soul of dancing ; both are
instinctive.

The greatest French poet after Villon, the most dis-
reputable and the most creative poet in French
literature, the greatest artist in French verse, and,
after Verlaine, the most passionate, perverse, lyrical,
visionary, and intoxicating of modern poets, comes
Baudelaire, infinitely more perverse, morbid, exotic
than these other poets. In his verse there is a deliberate science of sensual perversity, which has something
almost monachal in its accentuation of vice with
horror, in its passionate devotion to passions. Baudelaire brings every complication of taste, the exaspera-
tion of perfumes, the irritant of cruelty, the very
odours and colours of corruption to the creation and
adornment of a sort of religion, in which an eternal
mass is served before a veiled altar. There is no confession, no absolution, not a prayer is permitted which
is not set down in the ritual. With Verlaine, however
often love may pass into sensuality, to whatever
length sensuality may be hurried, sensuality is never
more than the malady of love.

The great epoch in French literature which preceded this epoch was that of the offshoot of Romanticism which produced Baudelaire, Flaubert, the Goncourts, Zola, and Leconte de Lisle. Even Baudelaire, in whom the spirit is always an uneasy guest at the orgy of life, had a certain theory of Realism which tortures many of his poems into strange, metallic shapes and fills them with irritative odours, and disturbs them with a too deliberate rhetoric of the flesh. Flaubert, the greatest novelist after Balzac, the only impeccable novelist who ever lived, was resolute to be the creator of a world in which art—formal art—was the only escape from the burden of reality. It was he who wrote to Baudelaire, who had sent him *Les Fleurs du Mal :* " I devoured your volume from one end to another, read it over and over again, verse by verse, word by word, and all I can say is it pleases and enchants me. You overwhelm me with your colours. What I admire most in your book is its perfect art. You praise flesh without loving it."

There is something Oriental in Baudelaire's genius ; a nostalgia that never left him after he had seen the East : there where one finds hot midnights, feverish days, strange sensations ; for only the East, when one has lived in it, can excite one's vision to a point of ardent ecstasy. He is the first modern poet who gave to a calculated scheme of versification a kind of secret and sacred joy. He is before all things the artist, always sure of his form. And his rarefied imagination aided him enormously not only in the perfecting of his verse and prose, but in making him create the criticism of modern art.

Next after Villon, Baudelaire is the poet of Paris.
Like a damned soul (to use one of his imaginary
images) he wanders at nights, an actual *noctambule*,
alone or with Villiers, Gautier, in remote quarters, sits
in cafés, goes to casinos, the *Rat Mort*. " The Wind of
Prostitution " (I quote his words) torments him, the
sight of hospitals, of gambling houses, the miserable
creatures one comes on in certain quarters, even the
fantastic glitter of lamplights. All this he needs : a
kind of intense curiosity, of excitement, in his fre-
quentation of these streets, comes over him, like one
who has taken opium. And this is only one part of
his life, he who lived and died solitary, a confessor of
sins who has never told the whole truth, *le mauvais
moins* of his own sonnet, an ascetic of passion, a hermit
of the brothel.

He is the first who ever related things in the modulated tone of the confessional and never assumed an
inspired air. The first also who brings into modern
literature the chagrin that bites at our existence like
serpents. He admits to his diabolical taste, not quite
exceptional in him ; one finds it in Petronius, Rabelais,
Balzac. In spite of his magnificent *Litanies de Satan*,
he is no more of the satanical school than Byron.
Yet both have the same sardonic irony, the delight of
mystification, of deliberately irritating solemn people's
convictions. Both, who died tragically young, had
their hours of sadness, when one doubts and denies
everything ; passionately regretting youth, turning
away, in sinister moods, in solitude, from that too
intense self-knowledge that, like a mirror, shows the
wrinkles on our cheeks.

IV

BAUDELAIRE, whose acquaintance with English
was perfect, was thrilled in 1846 when he read
certain pages of Poe ; he seemed to see in his prose a
certain similarity in words and thoughts, even in ideas,
as if he himself had written some of them ; these pages
of a prose-writer whom he named " the master of the
horrible, the prince of mystery." For four years he
set himself to the arduous task of translating the prose
of a man of genius, whom he certainly discovered for
France and for French readers. And his translation
is so wonderful that it is far and away finer than a
marvellous original. His first translation was printed
in *Le Liberté de Pensée* in July, 1848, and he only
finished his translations at the end of sixteen years. In
1852 the *Revue de Paris* printed his *Edgar Allan Poe ; sa
Vie et ses Ouvrages.* His translations came in this order :
Histoires Extraordinaires (1856, which I have before
me) ; *Nouvelles Histoires Extraordinaires* (1857, which I
also possess) ; *Aventures d'Arthur Gordon Pym* (1858) ;
Eureka (1864) ; *Histoires Grotesques et Sérieuses* (1865).

One knows the fury with which (in 1855) he set
himself the prodigious task of translating one of Poe's
stories every day ; which, to one's amazement, he
actually did. Always he rages over his proofs, over
those printers' devils, an accursed race ; every proof
is sent back to the printing press, revised ; underlined,
covered in the margins with imperative objurgations,

written with an angry hand and accentuated with
notes of exclamation. Swinburne shared the same
fate. He writes to Chatto a violent letter on the in-
competence of printers : " their scandalous negli-
gence," " ruinous and really disgraceful blunders,"
" numberless wilful errors," written in a state of perfect frenzy. " These damned printers," he cries at
them, as Baudelaire did ; " who have done their
utmost to disfigure my book. The appearance of the
pages is disgraceful—a chaos." And he actually writes
one letter to complain of a dropped comma !

The *Notes Nouvelles sur Edgar Poe* of 1857 are infinitely finer than those of 1856. He begins with :
Littérature de décadence ! and with a paradox, of his
invention, of the Sphynx without an enigma. *Genus
irritabile vatum !* a Latin phrase for the irritable race
of artists, is irrefutable, and certainly irrefutable are
all Baudelaire's arguments, divinations, revelations of
Poe's genius and of Poe's defects.

Poe's genius has been generally misunderstood. He
gave himself to many forms of misconception : by his
eccentricities, his caprices, his fantastic follies, his
natural insolence, his passionate excitations (mostly
imaginary), his delinquencies in regard to morals, his
over-acute sensibility, his exasperating way of exasperating the general public he hated, his analysing
problems that had defied any living writer's ingenuity
to have compassed (as in his detective stories) ; above
all, his almost utter alienation from that world he
lived in, dreamed in, never worshipped, died in.

And he remains still a kind of enigma ; in spite of
the fact that the most minute details of his life are

known, and that he never outlived his reputation. Yes, enigmatical in various points : as to his not giving even the breath of life to the few ghosts of women who cross his pages ; of never diving very deeply into any heart but his own. Are not most of his men malign, perverse, atrocious, abnormal, never quite normal, evocations of himself ? From Dupin to Fortunato, from the Man in the Crowd to the Man in the Pit, from Prince Prospero to Usher, are not these *revenants*, in the French sense ?

There is something demoniacal in his imagination ; for Poe never, I might say, almost never, lets his readers have an instant's rest ; any more than the Devil lets his subjects have any actual surcease of torment. Yet, as there is a gulf between Good and Evil, no one, by any chance, falls into the abyss.

Poe, of course, writes with his nerves, and therefore only nervous writers have ever understood him. It is Baudelaire, the most nervous of modern writers, who says of Poe that no one, before him, had affirmed imperturbably the natural wickedness of man. Yet this statement is a paradox ; a lesser paradox is that man is originally perverse ; for all are not *nés marqués pour le mal ?*

Poe is not a great critic ; he says certain unforgettable things, with even an anticipation of the work of later writers. " *I know*," he says, " that indefiniteness is an element of the true music—I mean of the true musical expression. Give it any undue decision—imbue it with any very determinate tone—and you deprive it at once of its ethereal, its ideal, its intrinsic and essential character " Where he is great is where he writes : " I have a pure contempt for mere prejudice and conventionality ; " and mostly where he defines himself. " Nor is there an instance to be discovered, among all I have published, of my having set forth, either in praise or censure, a single opinion upon any critical topic of moment, without attempting, at least, to give it authority by something that wore the semblance of a reason."

His fault is that he is too lenient to woman poets who never merited that name and to men of mere talent ; yet he annihilates many undeserved reputations ; perhaps, after all, " thrice slain." No one pointed out the errors in Mrs. Browning's verses as he id ; her affectations such as " God's possibles ; " her often inefficient rhythm ; her incredibly bad rhymes. Yet, for all this, he, whose ear as a poet was almost perfect, made the vile rhyme of " vista " with "sister," that raised the righteous wrath of Rossetti.

In his essay on Hawthorne, he warns one from a certain heresy. " The deepest emotion aroused within us by the happiest allegory, as an allegory, is a very imperfectly satisfied sense of the writer's ingenuity in overcoming a difficulty we should have preferred his not having attempted to overcome." But it is on pages 196–198 of his *Marginalia* that he gives his final statement in regard to Verse, the Novel, and the Short Story ; so far as these questions have any finality. As, for instance, how the highest genius uses his powers in " the composition of a rhymed poem, not to exceed in length what might be perused in an hour." As for the Story, it has this immense advantage over a novel that its brevity adds to the intensity of the effect ;

that " Beauty can be better treated in the poem, but that one can use terror and passion and horror as artistic means." Poe was a master of the grotesque, of the extraordinary, never of the passionate.

There is an unholy magic in some of his verse and prose ; in his hallucinations, so real and so unreal ; his hysterics, his sense of the contradiction between the nerves and the spirit ; in his scientific analyses of terrible, foreseen effects, where generally the man of whom he writes is driven into evil ways. For did he not state this axiom : " A good writer has always his last line in view when he has written his first line ? " This certainly was part of his *métier*, made of combinations and of calculations.

I read somewhere, " There is nothing wonderful in ' The Raven.' " It is really a *tour de force ;* even if the metre is not invented, he invented the inner double rhymes, and the technique is flawless. It has Black Magic in it ; the unreality of an intoxication ; a juggler's skill ; it will be always his most famous poem. In his analysis of these verses, does not Poe undervalue the inspiration that created them ? Yes, by an amusing vanity. And, as Baudelaire says : " A little charlatanism is always permitted to a man of genius, and it doesn't suit him badly. It is like the rouge on the cheeks of a woman actually fair, a new form of seasoning for the spirit."

There was too much of the woman in the making of Poe, manly as he was in every sense. He had no strength of will, was drawn from seduction to seduction ; had not enough grip on his constitution to live wisely, to live well. He drifted, let himself be drifted.

He had no intention of ruining himself, yet ruined he was, and there was nothing that could have saved him. Call it his fate or his evil star, he was doomed inevitably to an early death. *Pas de chance !* Yes—let one suppose—had he himself chosen the form of his death, he might have desired to die like the sick women in his pages—*mourant de maux bizarres*.

Baudelaire, the most scrupulous of the men of letters of our age, spent his whole life in writing one book of verse (out of which all French poetry has come since his time), one book of prose in which prose becomes a fine art, some criticism which is the sanest, subtlest, and surest which his generation produced, and a translation which is better than a marvellous original. Often an enigma to himself, much of his life and of his adventures and of his experiences remain enigmatical. I shall choose one instance out of many ; that is to say, what was the original of his dedication of *L'Heautimoromenos* in *Les Fleurs du Mal*, and of his dedication of *Les Paradis Artificiels* to a woman whose initials are J. G. F. ?

The poem was first printed in *L'Artiste*, May 10, 1857, together with two other poems, all equally strange, extraordinary, and enigmatical : *Franciscae Meae Laudes*, and *L'Irrémédiable*. The Latin verses, composed, not in the manner of Catullus, but in a metre that belongs to the late Decadent poets of the Middle Ages, are as magnificent as inspired, and are written really in modern Latin. This is the Dedication : *Vers composés pour une modiste érudite et dévote*. The verses are musical and luxurious. He sings of this delicious woman who absolves one's sins,

who has drunk of the waters of Lethe, who has spoken
as a star, who has learned what is vile, who has been
in his hunger an hostel, in his night a torch, and who
has given him divine wine. The second, that has the
woman's initials, is founded, as to its name, on the
comedy of Terence, *The Self-Tormentor*, where, in fact,
the part of Menedemas, the self-tormentor, rises to
almost tragic earnestness, and reminds one occasion-
ally of Shakespeare's *Timon of Athens*. Nor are
Baudelaire's verses less tragic. It is the fiercest confession in the whole of his poems in regard to himself
and to women. He strikes her with hate, cannot
satiate his thirst of her lips ; is a discord in her vora-
cious irony that bites and shakes himself ; she is in
his voice, in his blood (like poison), and he is her sinister
mirror. He is the wound and the knife, the limbs, and
the wheel ; he is of his own heart the vampire condemned in utter abandonment to an eternal laughter.

The third is a hideous nightmare when Idea and
Form and Being fall into the Styx, where a bewitched
wretch fumbles in a place filled with reptiles ; where
a damned man descends without a lamp eternal stair-
cases on which he has no hold ; and these are symbols
of an irremediable fortune which makes one think that
the Devil always does whatever he intends to do. At
the end a heart becomes his mirror ; and before the
Pit of Truth shines an infernal and ironical lighthouse,
that flashes with satanical glances and is : *La Conscience dans le Mal !*

In *Les Fleurs du Mal* (1857), a copy of which, signed
in Baudelaire's handwriting, is before me on the desk
where I write these lines, I find that the two first poems

I have mentioned follow each other in pages 123–127, and I feel certainly inclined to attribute those three poems to the same inspiration. Compare, for example, " Puits de Vérité " with *Piscina plena virtutis ;* " Dans un Styx bourbeux " with *Sicat beneficum Lethe ;* " Tailler les eaux de la souffrance " with *Labris vocem redde mutis !* " Au fond d'un cauchemar énorme " with " Je suis de mon cœur le vampire." And, " Je suis le sinister miroir " with " Qu'un cœur devenu son miroir." Compare also the dedication to the Latin verses " A une modiste érudite et dévote " with, in the dedication of *Les Paradis,* " une qui tourne maintenant tous ses regards vers le ciel." His reason for writing Latin verses for and to a dressmaker is evident enough : a deliberate deviation from the truth, a piece of sublime casuistry. One must also note this sentence : " Le calembour lui-même, quand il traverse ces pédantesques bégaiements, ne joue-t-il pas la grâce sauvage et baroque de l'enfance ? " And again, when he writes : " Words, taken in quite a new acceptation of their meaning, reveal the charming uneasiness of the Barbarian of the North who kneels before a Roman Beauty ; " this sentence certainly is only comprehensible if one realizes that it was written for J. G. F. Finally, take these two lines, which seem to prove satisfactorily the truth of my attribution :

> *In nocte mea taberna.*
> *Flambeau des grâces sataniques.*

I return to my copy of *Les Paradis Artificiels* (1860). The dedication to J. G. F. begins : *"Ma chère amie,* Common-sense tells us that terrestrial things have but a faint existence, and that actual reality is found

LES

PARADIS

ARTIFICIELS

OPIUM ET HASCHISCH

PAR

CHARLES BAUDELAIRE

PARIS
POULET-MALASSIS ET DE BROISE
LIBRAIRES-ÉDITEURS

97, rue Richelieu et passage Mirès

—

1861

Traduction et reproduction réservées.

only in dreams. Woman is fatally suggestive ; she
lives with another life than her proper one ; she lives
spiritually in the imaginations that she haunts.

" Besides, it seems to me there is little enough reason
why this dedication should be understood. Is it even
necessary, for the writer's satisfaction, that any kind
of book ought to be understood, except by him or by
her for whom it has been composed ? Is it, indeed,
indispensable that it has been written for *any one ?*
I have, for my part, so little taste for the living world
that, like certain sensible and stay-at-home women
who send, I am told, their letters to imaginary friends
by the post, I would willingly write only for the dead.

" But it is not to a dead woman that I dedicate this
little book ; it is to one who, though ill, is always
active and living in me, and who now turns her eyes
in the direction of the skies, that realm of so many
transfigurations. For, just as in the case of a redoubt-
able drug, a living being enjoys the privilege of being
able to draw new and subtle pleasures even from
sorrow, from catastrophe, and from fatality.

" You will see in this narrative a man who walks in
a sombre and solitary fashion, plunged in the moving
flood of multitudes, sending his heart and his thoughts
to a far-off Electra who so long ago wiped his
sweating forehead and *refreshed his lips parched by
fever ;* and you will divine the gratitude of another
Orestes, whose nightmares you have so often watched
over, and whose unendurable slumbers you dissipated,
with a light and tender hand."

I have to say that in the last sentences I have trans-
lated Baudelaire uses " tu " instead of " vous," and

that he does the same in his Latin verses and in the
verses next after it. The question still remains : who
was the woman of the initials ?

What is certainly not a solution of the unfathom-
able mystery of this enigmatical woman, but which is,
in a certain sense, a clue, I find on pages 55–67 of the
book I have referred to, a narrative that seems more
than likely to have been hers. He says this to make
one understand better the mixture of dreams and
hallucinations in haschisch, as having been sent him
by a woman : " It is a woman, rather a mature woman,
curious, of an excitable spirit, who, having yielded to
the temptation of using the drug, describes her visions."
These are superb and fantastic visions, written by an
imaginative, sensitive, and suggestive woman. She
begins : " However bizarre and astonishing are these
sensations that intoxicated my folly for twelve hours
(twelve or twenty ? I don't know which) I shall never
return to them. The spiritual excitement is too vivid,
the fatigue too much to endure, and, to say all, in this
childish enchantment I find something criminal." She
adds : " I have heard that the enthusiasm of poets
and of creators is not unlike what I have experienced,
in spite of the fact that I have always imagined that
such men whose delight is to move us ought to be of a
really calm temperament ; but if poetical delirium has
any resemblance with what a little teaspoon full of
drugged jam has given me, I think that all such pleasures cost dear to poets, and it is not without a certain
prosaic satisfaction that I return to real life."

In these sentences Baudelaire gives one a certain
clue as to the identity of this woman. " But, above

all, observe that in this woman's story the hallucination is of a bastard kind, and whose reason of being is to be an exterior spectacle ; the mind is no more than a mirror where the surrounding environment is transformed in an extraordinary fashion. Besides, we see intervene what I must call the moral hallucination : the subject believes he is subjected to an expiation, but the feminine temperament, which is little accustomed to analysis, does not permit itself to note the singularly optimistic character of this hallucination. The benevolent regard of the Olympian Divinities is poetized by a kind of varnish essentially *haschischin*. I cannot say that this woman has escaped from the sense of remorse ; but that her thoughts, momentarily turned in the direction of melancholy and of regret, have returned to their former sensibility."

I need not take into account his Latin learning, his Jesuitical casuistry, his erudite reference to Electra ; nor his ambiguous but not enigmatical linking together of the names of Orestes and Electra, to make it positively certain that the three poems were inspired by the same woman to whom *Le Paradis* is dedicated. Like Orestes, he might have desired vengeance, as the fugitive did for his murdered father ; she, like Electra, might have said, in Sophocles' words : " And my wretched couch in yonder house of woe knows well, ere now, how I keep the watches of the night—how often I bewail my hapless sin." I find exactly the same feeling in the sentences I have given of the dedication as in Electra's speech : nights of weariness and of lamentation. And Orestes exiled is ever in her thoughts. Why not in J. G. F.'s ?

In 1859 Poulet-Malassis printed : *Théophile Gautier, par Charles Baudelaire ;* a book of 68 pages ; certainly full of perfect praise, as only one so infinitely greater than the writer he writes about was capable of giving. The first question the oriental-looking Gautier asked him was : " Do you love dictionaries ? " The reply was instant : " Yes ! " As a matter of fact, Gautier knew every word in the French language, even *l'Argot.*

Now, as Baudelaire defines the genius of Balzac supremely (more than he ever could have defined the incomparable talents of Gautier), I leave it to Swinburne to speak for me of Baudelaire and of Balzac.

" Not for the first," he says, in his *Study of Shakespeare,* " and probably not for the last time I turn, with all confidence, as well as with reverence, for illustration and confirmation of my own words, to the exquisite critical genius of a long honoured and long lamented fellow-craftsman. The following admirable and final estimate of the more special element or peculiar quality in the intellectual force of Honoré de Balzac could only have been taken by the inevitable intuition and rendered by the subtlest eloquence of Charles Baudelaire. Nothing could more aptly and perfectly illustrate the definition indicated in my text between unimaginative realism and imaginative reality.

" ' I have been many a time astonished that to pass for an observer should be Balzac's great title to fame. To me it had always seemed that it was his chief merit to be a visionary, and a passionate visionary. All his characters are gifted with the ardour of life which animated himself. All his fictions are as deeply coloured as dreams. From the highest of the aris-

tocracy to the lowest of the mob, all the actors in his
Human Comedy are keener after living, more active
and cunning in their struggles, more staunch in en-
durance of misfortune, more ravenous in enjoyment,
more angelic in devotion, than the comedy of the real
world shows them to us.   In a word, every one in
Balzac, down to the very scullions, has genius.   Every
mind is a weapon loaded to the muzzle with will.   It
is actually Balzac himself.   And as all beings of the
outer world presented themselves to his mind's eye in
a strong relief and with a telling expression, he has
given a convulsive action to his figures ; he has
blackened their shadows and intensified their lights.
Besides, his prodigious love of detail, the outcome of
an immoderate ambition to see everything, to bring
everything to light, to guess everything, to make
others guess everything, obliged him to set down more
forcibly the principal lines so as to preserve the per-
spective of the whole.   He reminds me of some lines
of those etchers who are never satisfied with the biting-
in of their outlines, and transform into very ravines
the main scratches of the plate.   From this astonishing
natural disposition of mind wonderful results have
been produced.   But this disposition is generally
defined as Balzac's great fault.   More properly speaking, it is exactly his great distinctive quality.   But
who can boast of being so happily gifted, and of being
able to apply a method which may permit him to
invest—and that with a sure hand—what is purely
trivial with splendour and imperial purple ?   Who can
do this ?   Now, he who does not, to speak the truth,
does no great thing.' "

E

V

" I AM far from sure," said Paul Verlaine to me in
Paris, " that the philosophy of Villiers de l'Isle-
Adam will not one day become the formula of our
century." Fundamentally, the belief of Villiers is the
belief common to all Eastern mystics. And there is in
everything he wrote a strangeness, certainly both instinctive and deliberate, which seems to me to be the
natural consequences of his intellectual pride. It is
part of his curiosity in souls—as in the equally sinister
curiosity of Baudelaire—to prefer the complex to the
simple, the perverse to the straightforward, the
ambiguous to either. His heroes are incarnations of
spiritual pride, and their tragedies are the shock of
spirit against matter, the temptation of spirit by
spiritual evil. They are on the margins of a wisdom
too great for their capacity ; they are haunted by dark
powers, instincts of ambiguous passions. And in the
women his genius created there is the immortal weariness of beauty ; they are enigmas to themselves ; they
desire, and know not why they refrain ; they do good
and evil with the lifting of an eyelid, and are guilty
and innocent of all the sins of the earth.

Villiers wrote these significant sentences in the preface to *La Révolte* (1870) : " One ought to write for
the entire world. Besides, what does justice matter
to us ? He who from his very birth does not contain

54

M. Grandguillot
Rédacteur en
Chef du
Constitutionnel.

Mon cher ami,

Une note paraît demain ou
après demain au Constitutionnel
il est convenable que M. Grandguillot
reçoive un exemplaire. M. Zimmer
auteur de la Réclame, fait actuelle-
ment partie de la Rédaction du
Constitutionnel.

Et les ép. sur fil ?
Et Santien, qui se plaint ?
Et Ducamp ?
Et moi ?

Tout à vous.
C. B.

in himself his proper glory shall never know the real significance of this word." In the literature of the fantastic there are few higher names than that of the Comte de Villiers de l'Isle-Adam—a writer whose singular personality and work render him perhaps the most extraordinary figure in the contemporary world of letters. The descendant of a Breton house of fabulous antiquity, his life has been, like his works, a paradox, and an enigma. He has lived, as he says somewhere, " par politesse," ceaselessly experimenting upon life, perhaps a little too consciously, with too studied an extravagance of attitude, but at least brilliantly, and with dramatic contrasts. An immense consciousness of his own genius, a pride of race, a contempt, artistic and aristocratic, of the common herd, and, more especially, of the *bourgeois* multitude of letters and of life : it is to moods of mind like these, permanent with him, that we must look for the source of that violent and *voulu* eccentricity which mars so much of his work, and gives to all of it so disdainful an air. It is unfortunate, I think, when an artist condescends so far as to take notice of the Philistine element in which an impartial Providence has placed him. These good people we have always with us, and I question if any spiritual arms are of avail against them. They are impervious, impalpable ; they do not know when they are hit. But to Villiers " les gens de sens commun " are an incessant preoccupation. He is aware of his failure of temper, and writes at the head of a polemical preface, *Genus irritabile vatum*.

In considering the work of Villiers I am brought face to face with a writer who seems to be made up of contradictions. Any theory, if it be at all precise, must proceed by making exceptions. Here is a writer who is at once a transcendentalist and a man of the world, a cynic and a believer in the things of the spirit. He is now Swift, now Bernadin de St. Pierre, now Baudelaire or Heine. In reading him you pass from exaltation to buffoonery with the turn of a page, and are never quite sure whether he is speaking seriously or in jest. Above all, everywhere there is irony ; and the irony is of so fine a point, and glances in so many directions, that your judgment is distracted, interrupted, contradicted, and confused in a whirlwind of conflicting impressions.

Villiers has written much. The volume of *Contes Cruels* (published in 1880) includes, I believe, work of many periods ; it contains specimens of every style its author has attempted, and in every kind the best work that he has done. The book as a whole is a masterpiece, and almost every separate tale is a masterpiece. I can think of no other collection of tales in any language on which so various and finely gifted a nature has lavished itself ; none with so wide a gamut of feeling, none which is so Protean a manifestation of genius. The *Tales* of Edgar Poe alone surpass it in sheer effect, the *Twice-Told Tales* of Hawthorne alone approach it in variety of delicate sensation ; both, compared with its shifting and iridescent play of colours, are but studies in monochrome. Around this supreme work we may group the other volumes. *La Révolte*, a drama in one act in prose, represented at the Vaudeville, May 6th, 1870, has something of the touch of certain *Contes Cruels ;* it is, at least, not unworthy of a place near them. *L'Eve Future* (1886), that most immense and ferocious of pleasantries, is simply one of the scientific burlesques of the *Contes* swollen out into a huge volume, where it is likely to die of plethora. The volume of the same year, called after its first tale *L'Amour Suprême*, attempts to be a second set of *Contes Cruels ;* it has nothing of their distinction, except in *Akëdysséril. Tribulat Bonhomet*, which appeared in 1887—" une bouffonnerie énorme et sombre, couleur du siècle," as the author has called it— is largely made up of an " Étude physiologique " published in 1867. In the two later volumes, *Histoires Insolites* (1888) and *Nouveaux Contes Cruels* (1889), there are occasional glimpses of the early mastery, as in the fascinating horror of *La Torture par l'Experance*, and the delicate cynicism of *Les Amies de Pension*. As for the prose drama in five acts, *Le Nouveau Monde* (1876), which had the honour of gaining a prize—" une médaille honorifique, une somme de dix mille francs même, d'autres seductions encore " —there is little in it of the true Villiers ; a play with striking effects, no doubt, movement, surprises, a grandiose air ; but what would you have of a " prize poem " ? It was acted at one of the theatres at Paris in 1883, under the auspices of the dilettante Comte d'Orsay, and it had a very gratifying " literary " success. Such, omitting the early works, of which I have every first edition, and the numerous volumes of which the titles and no more have been published, are the works we have before us from which to study " peut-être le seul des hommes de notre géneration qui ait eu en lui l'étincelle du génie "—as Catulle

Mendès, ever generous in his literary appreciation of friend and foe, has said in that charming book, *La Légende du Parnasse Contemporaine*. I shall speak chiefly of the *Contes Cruels*, and I shall try to classify them after a fashion, in order to approach one after another the various sides of this multiform and many-sided genius.

First and before all, Villiers is a humorist, and he is a humorist who has no limitations, who has command of every style, who has essayed every branch of the literature of the fantastic. There are some half-dozen of tales—all contained in the *Contes Cruels*—which, for certain of the rarest qualities of writing—subtleties, delicate perversities, exquisite complexities of irony essentially modern—can be compared, so far as I know, with nothing outside the *Petits Poèmes en Prose* of Baudelaire. *Les Demoiselles de Bienfilâtre, Maryelle, Sentimentalisme, Le Convive des Dernières Fêtes, La Reine Ysabeau*—one might add the solitary poem inserted, jewel amid jewels, amongst the prose—these pieces, with which one or two others have affinities of style though not of temper, constitute a distinct division of Villiers' work. They are all, more or less, studies in modern love, supersubtle and yet perfectly finished little studies, so light in touch, manipulated with so delicate a finesse, so exquisite and unerring in tact, that the most monstrous paradoxes, the most incredible assumptions of cynicism, become possible, become acceptable. Of them all I think the master-piece is *Les Demoiselles de Bienfilâtre ;* and it is one of the most perfect little works of art in the world. The mockery of the thing is elemental ; cynicism touches its zenith. It becomes tender, it becomes sublime. A perversion simply monstrous appears, in the infantine simplicity of its presentment, touching, credible, heroic. The edge of laughter is skirted by the finest of inches ; and, as a last charm, one perceives, through the irony itself—the celestial, the elementary irony—a faint and sweet perfume as of a perverted odour of sanctity. The style has the delicacy of the etcher's needle. From beginning to end every word has been calculated, and every word is an inspiration. No other tale quite equals this supreme achievement ; but in *Maryelle*, in *Sentimentalisme*, and the others there is the same note, and a perfection often only less absolute. *Maryelle* and *Sentimentalisme* are both studies in a special type of woman, speculations round a certain strange point of fascination ; and they render that particular type with the finest precision. The one may be called a comedy, the other a tragedy. The experiences they record are comic (in the broad sense), certainly, and tragic to the men who undergo them ; and in both, under the delicate lightness of the style— the gentle, well-bred, *disengaged* tone of a *raconteur* without reserve or after-thought, or with all that scrupulously hid—there is a sort of double irony, a criss-cross and intertexture of meanings and sugges- tions, a cynicism which turns, in spite of itself, to poetry, or a poetry which is really the other side of cynicism. *La Reine Ysabeau* and *Le Convive des Dernières Fêtes* sound a new note, the note of horror. The former stands almost by itself in the calm cruelty of its style, the singular precision of the manner in which its atrocious complication of love, vengeance,

and fatality is unrolled before our eyes—the something
enigmatical in the march of the horrible narrative told
almost with tenderness. Its serenity is the last refinement of the irony with which this incredible episode
arraigns the justice of things. From the parenthesis
of the first sentence to the " Priez pour eux," every
touch tells, and every touch is a surprise. Very
different, and yet in certain points akin to it, is the
strange tale of *Le Convive des Dernières Fêtes*, perhaps,
after the more epic chronicle of *La Reine Ysabeau*, the
finest of Villiers' tales of enigmatical horror. Quietly
as the tale is told, full as it is of complications, and
developed through varying episodes, it holds us as the
Ancient Mariner held the wedding guest. It is with a
positive physical sensation that we read it, an instinctive shiver of fascinated and terrified suspense. There
is something of the same *frisson* in the latter part of
Tribulat Bonhomet, and in the marvellous little study
in the supernatural *L'Intersigne*, one of the most im-
pressive of Villiers' works. But here the sensation is
not due to effects really out of nature ; and the element
of horror—distinct and peculiar as is the impression it
leaves upon the mind—is but one among the many
elements of the piece. In these thirty pages we have
a whole romance, definitely outlined characters, all
touched with the same *bizarrerie*—the execution-mad
Baron, Clio la Cendrée, Antoine Chantilly, and
Susannah Jackson ; the teller of the tale, the vague
C., and the fantastic Doctor. Narrow as is the space,
it is surcharged with emotion ; a word, a look, a smile,
a personal taste, is like the touching of an electric
button ; and, indeed, it is under the electric light that

one fancies these scenes to enact themselves—scenes
which have as little in common with mere daylight
as their personages with average humanity. It is a
world in which the virtues have changed their names,
and coquette with the vices; and in masque and
domino one is puzzled to distinguish the one from the
other. It is a world of exquisite, delicately depraved
beings trembling with sensibility. Irony is their
breath of life, paradox their common speech. And the
wizard who has raised these ghosts seems to stand
aside and regard them with a sarcastic smile.

What is Villiers' view of life? it may occur to us to
ask; is he on the side of the angels? That is a question it is premature to answer; I have to look next
on another and a widely different aspect of the fantastic edifice of his work.

The group of tales I have been considering reveals
the humorist in his capacity of ironical observer:
their wit is a purely impersonal mockery, they deal
with life from the point of view of the artist, and they
are pre-eminently artistic, free from any direct purpose
or preoccupation. In the pseudo-scientific burlesques,
and the kindred satires on ignorant and blatant
mediocrity, the smile of the Comic Muse has given
place to " Laughter holding both his sides; " absurdity caps absurdity, order and measure seem to be
flung to the winds, and in this new Masque of Anarchy
sharp blows are given, the jests are barbed, and they
fly not quite at random. " L'Esprit du siècle," says
Villiers, " ne l'oublions pas, est aux machines." And
it is in the mechanical miracles of modern science that
he has found a new and unworked and inexhaustible

field of satire. Jules Verne has used these new dis-
coveries with admirable skill in his tales of extravagant
wonder ; Villiers seizes them as a weapon, and in his
hands it becomes deadly, and turns back upon the
very age which forged it ; as a means of comedy, and
the comedy becomes soberly Rabelaisian, boisterous
and bitter at once, sparing nothing, so that he can
develop the deliberate plan of " an apparatus for the
chemical analysis of the last sigh," make a sober pro-
posal for the utilization of the sky as a means of
advertisement (*Affichage Céleste*), and describe in all its
detail and through all its branches the excellent invention of Bathybius Bottom, *La Machine à Gloire*,
a mechanical contrivance for obtaining dramatic
success with the expense and inconvenience of that
important institution, the Claque. In these wild and
whirling satires, which are at bottom as cold and
biting as Swift, we have a quite new variety of style,
a style of patchwork and grimaces. Familiar words
take new meanings, and flash through all the transformations of the pantomime before our eyes ; strange
words start up from forgotten corners ; words and
thoughts, never brought together since Babel, clash
and stumble into a protesting combination ; and in
the very aspect of the page there is something startling.
The absurdity of these things is so extreme, an absurdity so supremely serious, that we are carried almost
beyond laughter, and on what is by virtue of its
length the most important of the scientific burlesques,
L'Eve Future, it is almost impossible to tell whether
the author is really in sober earnest or whether the
whole thing is a colossal joke. Its 375 pages are

devoted to a painfully elaborate description of the manufacture, under the direction of the " très-illustre inventeur américain, M. Edison," of an *artificial woman !* No such fundamental satire, such ghastly exposure of " poor humanity," has been conceived since Swift. The sweep of it covers human nature, and its essential laughter breaks over the very elements of man. Unfortunately the book is much too long ; its own weight sinks it ; the details become wearisome, the seriousness of the absurdity palls.

So far we have had the humorist, a humorist who appears to be cynic to the backbone, cynic equally in the Parisian perversities of *Les Demoiselles de Bienfilâtre* and the scientific hilarity of *La Machine à Gloire.* But we have now to take account of one of those "exceptions" of which I spoke—work which has nothing of the humorist in it, work in which there is not a trace of cynicism, work full of spirituality and all the virtues. *Virginie et Paul* is a story of young love comparable only with that yet lovelier story, the magical chapter, in *Richard Feverel.* This Romeo and Juliet are both fifteen, and their little moment of lovers' chat, full of the poetry of the most homely and natural things, is brought before us in a manner so exquisitely true, so perfectly felt, that it is not even sentimental. Every word is a note of music, a song of nightingales among the roses—*per amica silentia lunœ*—and there is not a wrong note in it, no exaggeration, nothing but absolute truth and beauty. The strange and charming little romance of *L'Inconnue* is another of these tales of ingenuous love, full of poetry fresh from lovers' hearts, and with a delicate rhythmical effect in its carefully modulated style. *L'Amour Suprême*, a less perfect work of art, exhales the same aroma of tender and etherealized affection—an adoring and almost mystic love of the ideal incarnated in woman. In the bizarre narrative of *Véra*, which recalls the supernatural romances of Poe, there is again this strange spirituality of tone ; and in the dazzling prose poem of *Akēdyssēril*—transfigured prose glowing with Eastern colour, a tale of old-world passion full of barbaric splendour, and touched, for all its remoteness, with the human note—in this epic fragment, considered in France, I believe, to be, in style at least, Villiers' masterpiece, it is humanity transfigured in the light of the ideal that we contemplate. Humanity transfigured in the light of the ideal !—think for a moment of *Les Demoiselles de Bienfilâtre*, of *L'Analyse chimique du Dernier Soupir !* What, then, are we to believe ? Has Villiers two natures, and can he reconcile irreconciliable opposites ? Or if one is the real man, which one ? And what of the other ? What, in a word, is the true Villiers ? " For, as he thinketh in his heart, so is he."

The question is not a difficult one to answer ; it depends upon an elementary knowledge of the nature of that perfectly intelligible being, the cynic. The typical cynic is essentially a tender-hearted, sensitive idealist ; his cynicism is in the first instance a recoil, then, very often, a disguise. Most of us come into the world without any very great expectations, not looking for especial loftiness in our neighbours, not very much shocked if every one's devotion to the ideal is not on a level with, perhaps, ours. We go on our way, if not exactly "rejoicing," at least without positive discomfort. Here and there, however, a soul nurtured on dreams and nourished in the scorn of compromise finds its way among men and demands of them perfection. There is no response to the demand. Entranced by an inaccessible ideal, the poor soul finds that its devotion poisons for it all the wells of earth. And this is the birth of what we call a cynic. The cynic's progress is various, and seldom in a straight line. It is significant to find that in *La Révolte*, one of Villiers' comparatively early works, the irony has a perfectly serious point, and aims directly at social abuses. The tableau is a scene, an episode, taken straight from life, a piece of the closest actuality ; there is no display, no exaggeration, all is simple and straightforward as truth. The laughter in it is the broken-hearted laughter, sadder than tears, of the poet, the dreamer, before the spectacle of the world. It is obviously the work of one who is a mocker through his very passion for right and good, his sense of the infinite disproportion of things. Less obviously, but indeed quite really, is the enormous and almost aimless mockery of some of these tales of his the reverse of a love of men and a devotion to the good and the beautiful. Cynicism is a quality that develops, and when we find it planted in the brain of a humorist there is simply no accounting for the transformations through which it may run. Thus the gulf which seems to separate *Les Demoiselles de Bienfilâtre* from *L'Inconnue* is, after all, nothing but a series of steps. Nor is it possible for one who judges art as art to regret this series of steps ; for it is precisely his cynicism that has become the " note," the rarest quality, of this man of passionate and lofty genius ; it is as a cynic that he will live—a cynic who can be pitiless and tender, Rabelaisian and Heinesque, but imaginative, but fantastically poetical, always.

GUSTAVE COURBET, 1848

VI

L *ES Paradis Artificiels : Opium et Haschisch* (1860),
which I have before me, is the most wonderful
book that Baudelaire ever wrote. It has that astonishing logic which he possessed supremely, which
unravels, with infinite precautions, every spider's web
of this seductive drug, which enslaves the imagination,
which changes the will, which turns sounds into
colours, colours into sounds ; which annihilates space
and time ; and, often at its crises, even one's own
individuality. To Baudelaire, as to me, it has, and
had, the divinity of a sorcerous, a dangerous, an in-
sidious mistress. It produces morbid effects on one's
senses ; wakens mysterious visions in our half-closed
eyes. And this, like every form of intoxication, is
mysterious, malign, satanical, diabolical. And, sub-
jugated by it, part of oneself is dominated, so that, in
Baudelaire's words : *Il a vouloir faire l'ange, il est
devenu une bête.*

With some this poison carries them to the verge of
the abyss, over which one looks fascinated by the
abrupt horror of the void. In some their ideas congeal :
even to the point of imagining oneself " a fragment of
thinking ice." One sits, as in a theatre, seeing a drama
acted on the stage, where one's senses perceive subtle
impressions, but vague, unreal, ghost-like ; where at
moments one's eyes envisage the infinite. " Then,"

67

says Baudelaire, " the grammar, the arid grammar
itself, becomes something like an evoked sorcery, the
words are alive again in flesh and in blood, the sub-
stantive, in its substantial majesty, the adjective, a
transparent vestment that clothes it and colours it
like a glacis, and the verb, angel of movement, that
gives the swing to the phrase."

With the hallucinations all exterior forms take on
singular aspects ; are deformed and transformed.
Then come the transpositions of ideas, with unaccount-
able analogies that penetrate the spirit. Even music,
heard or unheard, can seem voluptuous and sensual.
It is Baudelaire who speaks now, evokes an enchantment : " The idea of an evaporation, slow, successive,
eternal, takes hold of your spirit, and you soon apply
this idea to your proper thoughts, to your way of
thinking. By a singular equivocation, by a kind of
transportation, or of an intellectual *quid pro quo*, you
find yourself evaporating, and you attribute to your
pipe (in which you feel yourself crouching and heaped
together like tobacco) the strange faculty of *smoking
yourself*." The instant becomes eternity ; one is lucid
at intervals ; the hallucination is sudden, perfect, and
fatal. One feels an excessive thirst ; one subsides into
that strange state that the Orientals call *Kief*.

Certainly haschisch has a more vehement effect on
one than opium ; it is more troubling, more ecstatic,
more malign, malignant, insinuating, more evocative,
more visionary, more unseizable ; it lifts one across
infinite horizons, it carries us passionately over the
passionate waves of seas in storms—of unknown
storms on unseen seas—into not even eternities, nor

into chaos, nor into Heaven nor into Hell (though these may whirl before one's vision), but into incredible existences, over which no magician rules, over which no witch presides. It can separate ourselves from ourselves ; change our very shapes into shapeless images ; drown us in the deep depths of annihilation, out of which we slowly emerge ; bury us under the oldest roots of the earth ; give us death in life and life in death ; give us sleep that is not sleep, and waking dreams that are not waking dreams. There is nothing, human or inhuman, moral or immoral, that this drug cannot give us.

Yet, all the time, we know not what it takes from us, nor what deadly exchange we may have to give ; nor what intoxication can be produced beyond its intoxication ; nor if, as with Coleridge, who took opium, it might not become " almost a habit of the Soul."

Imagine a universe in disorder, peopled by strange beings, that have no relation with each other, whose speech one supposes is jargon ; where such houses as there are are built in different ways—none with straight lines, many in triangles ; where the animals are unlike ours, some smaller than ants ; where there are no churches, no apparent streets ; but innumerable brothels. When one sees fires the smoke goes downward ; flames leap out of the soil and turn into living serpents. Now one sees a serpent return into his proper flame. There seem to be no gods, nor idols nor priests nor shrines.

The seas storm the skies and swallow up Hell ; and all that lives and all that dies seems indistinguishable.

F

Suppose that—in an opium dream—Satan turns God. The soil might wither at his touch ; Lesbians lament the loss of Lesbianism ; and the word of God be abolished.

I have used the word vehement in regard to Haschisch. It violates the imagination, ravishes the senses ; can disturb one physically ; but never, if taken in measure, prove destructive. This green drug can create unheard-of excitations, exasperations ; can create contagious laughter, evoke comical images, supernatural and fantastic.

Now take a world created by Opium. The soil wavers, moves always, in void space ; a soil in which no seed nor weed grows. The men and women are veiled—none see their faces. There is light, but neither sun nor stars nor night. The houses have no windows ; inside are no mirrors ; but everywhere opium dens ; everywhere the smoke—incessant—of pipes ; everywhere a stench produced by opium and by their moral degradation. The streets are thick with grass ; such animals as there are are stupefied. In fact, this inexorably moving world that has no foundations exhales —worse than pestilence—an inexplicable stupefaction.

And, symbolical as it must be, these excitable poisons are to a certainty one of the most terrible means employed by the Prince of the Powers of the Air to enslave deplorable humanity ; but by no means to give him, what the drug can give him, the monstrous sense of the suddenness of space and time, as if one were hurled between them by two opposing whirlwinds.

Now appears suddenly the Women—furious, formidable—one calls Mephistophila, who having gazed on the Medusa becomes Medusa ; who, rouged and pale as the dead, gives one the idea of that eternal minute which must be hell. Her very name trails like a coffin-lid. Abnormal, she is sinister. She is one of my hallucinations. Can she ever count the countless sins she has committed ? Occult, she adores the Arcana. Her kisses on women's lips are cruel. Perhaps she is the modern Messalina. *Elle est l'impératrice blême d'un macabre Lesbos.*

She admits—I give here simply her confessions—to no abominations, nor does she specialize her vices. As certain of her damnation as of her existence—real, imaginary—she lives and loves and lies and forgives. She knows she has abandoned herself to all the impossible desires endured by such souls as hers, who expect annihilation. *Elle est la reine, pas présente, mais acceptée, de la cour des miracles femelles du Mal.*

She is not of those the Furies hate eternally, nor has she knowledge of man's mingled fates ; yet certain Circes have shown her how to weave webs of spiritual spiders ; she knows not where those are that turn the Wheels of Destiny. Whirlwinds have shaken her in her perfumed room as she lies in perfumed garments, considering her nakedness as sacred : she the impure, never the pure ! She is so tired of having ravished souls from bodies and bodies from souls, that all she desires is sleep, sleep without dreams. Did sleep ever come to those who most desired it ? Messalina, Helen of Troy, Faustina knew this ; dust has closed their lips, the very dust they have trodden under foot, the dust that knows not whither it is drifting : none thinking of the inevitable end.

Has not this poisonous drug shown to me, as to her, shadows hot from hell ? Not the shadows the sun casts on our figures as we walk on the grass ; not the moon's shadows that make mockery of us ; but the veritable heat and fire and flame and fumes of uttermost hell.

In her eyes persists an ardent and violent life, hateful and bestial. Depraved by insensible sensations, she imagines Caligula before her and maledictions not her own. I know her now in vision—she is more insatiable than Death—more ravenous after ravishment than Life. No vampire, no Lamia, she knows not that her body has been drenched with so many poisons that her breath might poison a man with one kiss. And now, now, her eyes are so weary, her eyeballs ache with such tortured nerves, that she desires nothing—nothing at all.

In the very essence of Haschisch I find a disordered Demon whose insanities make one's very flesh ache. Under his power symbols speak—you can become yourself a living symbol. Under its magic you can imagine black magic, and music can speak your passion : for is not music as passionate as man's love for woman, as a woman's love for a man ? It can turn your rhythm into its rhythm, can change every word into a sound, a word into a note of music : it cannot change the substance of your soul.

Finally, the drugged man admires himself inordinately ; he condemns himself, he glorifies himself ; he realizes his condemnation ; he becomes the centre of the universe, certain of his virtue as of his genius. Then, in a stupendous irony, he cries : *Je suis devenu*

Dieu ! One instant after he projects himself out of himself, as if the will of an intoxicated man had an efficacious virtue, and cries, with a cry that might strike down the scattered angels from the ways of the sky : *Je suis un Dieu !*

One of Baudelaire's profoundest sayings is : " Every perfect debauch has need of a perfect leisure : *Toute débauche parfaite a besoin d'un parfait loisir.*" He gives his definition of the magic that imposes on haschisch its infernal stigmata ; of the soul that sells itself in detail ; of the frantic taste for this adorable poison of the man whose soul he had chosen for these experiments, his own soul ; of how finally this hazardous spirit, driven, without being aware of it, to the edge of hell, testifies of its original grandeur.

VII

I

IN their later work all great poets use foreshorten-
ing. They get greater subtlety by what they
omit and suggest to the imagination. Browning, in
his later period, suggests to the intellect, and to that
only. Hence his difficulty, which is not a poetic difficulty ; not a cunning simplification of method like
Shakespeare's, who gives us no long speeches of un-
diluted undramatic poetry, but poetry everywhere like
life-blood.

Browning's whole life was divided equally between two things : love and art. He subtracted
nothing from the one by which to increase the other ;
between them they occupied his whole nature ; in
each he was equally supreme. *Men and Women* and
the love-letters are the double swing of the same
pendulum ; at the centre sits the soul, impelled and
impelling. Outside these two forms of his greatness
Browning had none, and one he concealed from the
world. It satisfied him to exist as he did, knowing
what he was, and showing no more of himself to those
about him than the outside of a courteous gentleman.
Nothing in him blazed through, in the uncontrollable
manner of those who are most easily recognized as
great men. His secret was his own, and still, to many,
remains so.

MANET, 1862

I have said above, of Browning : " His secret was
his own, and still, to many, remains so." Exactly the
same thing must be said of Baudelaire. He lived, and
died, secret ; and the man remains baffling, and will
probably never be discovered. But, in most of his
printed letters, he shows only what he cares to reveal
of himself at a given moment. In the letters, printed
in book form, that I have before me, there is much
more of the nature of confessions. Several of his
letters to his mother are heart-breaking ; as in his
agonized effort to be intelligible to her ; his horror of
her *curé* ; his shame in pawning her Indian shawl ;
his obscure certainty that the work he is doing is of
value, and that he ought not to feel shame. Then
comes his suggestion that society should adjust these
difficult balances. Again, in his ghastly confession
that he has only sent Jeanne seven francs in three
months ; that he is as tired of her as of his own life :
there is shown a tragic gift for self-observation and
humble truthfulness. It would have taken a very profound experience of life to have been a good mother
to Baudelaire : or she should have had a wiser *curé*.
Think of the *curé* burning the only copy of *Les Fleurs
du Mal* that Baudelaire had left in " papier d'Hol-
lande," and the mother acquiescing.

I give two quotations, which certainly explain themselves if they do not explain Baudelaire :

" I must leave home and not return there, except
in a more natural state of mind. I have just been re-
writing an article. The affair kept me so long that
when I went out I had not even the courage to return,
and so the day was lost. Last week I had to go out

and sleep for two days and nights in a hideous little hotel because I was spied on. I went out without any money for the simple reason that I had none.

" Imagine my perpetual laziness, which I hate profoundly, and the impossibility of going out on account of my perpetual want of money. After I had been seeking money for three days, on Monday night, exhausted with fatigue, with weariness and with hunger, I went into the first hotel I came on, and since then I have had to remain there, and for certain reasons. I am nearly devoured, eaten by this enforced idleness."

In a letter written in Brussels, March 9, 1868, he says : " I have announced the publication of three fragments : *Chateaubriand et la Dandysme littéraire, La Peinture didactique*, and *Les Fleurs du Mal jugées par l'auteur lui-même*. I shall add to these a refutation of an article of Janin, one on *Henri Heine et la jeunesse des poètes*, and the refutation of *La Préface de la vie de Jules César par Napoléon III*." Besides these, on the cover of his *Salon de* 1848 are announced : *"De la poésie moderne ; David, Guerin et Gerodet ; Les Limbes, poésies ; Catéchisme de la femme aimée."* On the paper cover of my copy of his *Théophile Gautier* (1861), under the title of " *Sous Presse*," are announced : *Opium et Haschisch, ou l'Idéal Artificiel* (which was printed in 1860 as *Les Paradis Artificiels : Opium et Haschisch*), *Curiosités Esthétiques* (which were printed in 1868) ; *Notices littéraires ;* and *Machiavel et Condorcet, dialogue philosophique*. Of these, *Les Limbes* appeared as *Les Fleurs du Mal* (1857) ; *Les Notices littéraires* at the end of *L'Art Romantique* (1868) ; none of the others were printed, nor do I suppose he had even the time to begin them.

He might have written on Machiavelli a prose dialogue as original, from the French point of view, as one of Landor's Imaginary Conversations, such as those between Plato and Diogenes, the two Ciceros, Leonora d'Este with Father Panigarole. Both had that satirical touch which can embody the spirit of an age or of two men in conversation. Both had a creative power and insight equal to that of the very greatest masters ; both had the power of using prose with a perfection which no stress of emotion is allowed to discompose. Only it seems to me that Baudelaire might have made the sinister genius, the calculating, cold observation of Machiavelli, who wrote so splendidly on Cesare Borgia, give vent to a tremendous satire on priests and Kings and Popes after the manner of Rabelais or of Aristophanes ; certainly not in the base and ignoble manner of Aretino.

It is lamentable to think how many things Baudelaire never did or never finished. One reason might have been his laziness, his sense of luxury, and, above all, his dissatisfaction with certain things he had hoped to do, and which likely enough a combination of poverty and of nerves prevented him from achieving. And as he looks back on the general folly incident to all mankind—his *bête noire*—on his lost opportunities, on his failures, a sack of cobwebs, a pack of gossamers, wave in the air before his vision ; and he wonders why he himself has not carved his life as those fanciful things have their own peculiar way of doing.

Baudelaire was inspired to begin *Mon Cœur mis à nu*

in 1863 by this paragraph he had read in Poe's *Marginalia*, printed in New York in 1856 : "If an ambitious man have a fancy to revolutionize, at one effort, the universal world of human thought, human opinion, and human sentiment, the opportunity is his own— the road to immortal renown lies straight open and unencumbered before him. All that he has to do is to write and publish a very little book. Its title should be simple—a few plain words—*My Heart Laid Bare.*"

With all his genius, Poe was never able to write a book of Confessions, nor was Baudelaire ever able to finish his. Poe, who also died tragically young, throws out a sinister hint in these last words : " No man *could* write it, even if he dared. The paper would shrivel and blaze at every touch of the fiery pen."

Baudelaire's Confessions are meant to express his inmost convictions, his most sacred memories, his hates and rages, the manner in which his sensations and emotions have fashioned themselves in his waking self ; to express that he is a stranger to the world and to the world's cults ; to express, also, as he says, that *ce livre tout rêvé sera un livre de rancunes.* It cannot in any sense be compared with the Confessions of Saint Augustine, of Rousseau, of Cellini, of Casanova. Still, Baudelaire had none of Rousseau's cowardice, none of Cellini's violent exultations over himself and the things he created : none of Casanova's looking back over his past life and his adventures : those of a man who did not live to write, but wrote because he had lived and when he could live no longer.

In Baudelaire's notes there is something that reminds me of Browning's lines :

> " Men's thoughts and loves and hates !
> Earth is my vineyard, these grew there ;
> From grapes of the ground, I made or marred
> My vintage."

For so much in these studies in sensations are the pro-
duct of a man who has both made and marred his
prose and poetical vintage. He analyses some of his
hideous pains ; and I cannot but believe—I quote
these words from a letter I have received from a man
of sensitive nerves—that he may have felt : " It *is* so
beautiful to emerge after the bad days that one is
almost glad to have been through them, and I can
quite truthfully say I am glad to have pain—it makes
one a connoisseur in sensations, and we only call it
pain because it is something that we don't understand."
Without having suffered intensely no poet can be a
real poet ; and without passion no poet is supreme.
And these lines of Shelley are not only meant for himself, but for most of us who are artists :

> " One who was as a nerve over which do creep
> The else unfelt oppressions of this earth."

There is also something Browning says of Shelley
which might be applied to Baudelaire's later years :
" The body, enduring tortures, refusing to give repose
to the bewildered soul, and the laudanum bottle
making but a perilous and pitiful truce between these
two." He was also subject to that state of mind in
which ideas may be supposed to assume the force of
sensations, through the confusion of thought with the

objects of thought, and excess of passion animating the creations of the imagination.

II

How very commonly we hear it remarked that such and such thoughts are beyond the compass of words. I do not believe that any thought, properly so called, is out of the reach of language. I fancy, rather, that where difficulty in expression is experienced, there is, in the intellect which experiences it, a want either of deliberateness or of method. For my own part, I have never had a thought which I could not set down in words with even more distinctness than that with which I conceived it : for thought is logicalized by the effort at written composition. There is, however, a class of fancies, of exquisite delicacy, which are not thoughts, and to which, as yet, I have found it absolutely impossible to adapt language. Yet, so entire is my faith in the power of words, that at times I have believed it possible to embody even the evanescences of fancies such as I have described. Could one actually do so, which would be to have done an original thing, such words might have compelled the heaven into the earth.

Some of these qualities Baudelaire finds in Gautier ; to my mind there are many more of these strange and occult qualities to be found in Baudelaire. I have said somewhere that there is no such thing, properly speaking, as a " natural " style ; and it is merely ignorance of the mental process of writing which sometimes leads one to say that the style of Swift is more natural than that of Ruskin. Pater said to me at Oxford that his

own *Imaginary Portraits* seemed to him the best
written of his books, which he qualified by adding :
" It seems to be the most *natural.*" I think then he
was beginning to forget that it was not natural to him
to be natural.

Gautier had a way of using the world's dictionary,
whose leaves, blown by an unknown wind, always
opened so as to let the exact word leap out of the
pages, adding the appropriate shades. Both writers
had an innate sense of " correspondences," and of a
universal symbolism, where the " sacredness " of every
word defends one from using it in a profane sense.
To realize the central secret of the mystics, from
Protagoras onwards, the secret which the Smaragdine
Tablet of Hermes betrays in its " As things are below,
so are they above ; " which Boehme has classed in his
teaching of " signatures ; " and which Swedenborg
has systematized in his doctrine of " correspondences,"
one arrives at Gérard de Nerval, whose cosmical visions
are at times so magnificent that he seems to be creating
myths, as, after his descent into hell, he plays the part
he imagines assigned to him in his astral influences.

Among these comes Hoffman. In his *Kreislerione*,
that Baudelaire read in the French translation I have
before me, printed in 1834, he says : " The musician
whose sense of music is conscious swims everywhere
across floods of harmony and melody. This is no vain
image, nor an allegory devoid of sense, such as com-
posers use when they speak of colours, of perfumes, of
the rays of the sun that appear like concords."
" Colour speaks," says Baudelaire, " in a voice evoca-
tory of sorcery ; animals and plants grimace ; per-

fumes provoke correspondent thoughts and memories. And when I think of Gautier's rapidity in solving all the problems of style and of composition, I cannot help remembering a severe maxim that he let fall before me in one of his conversations : ' Every writer who fails to seize any idea, however subtle and un-expected he supposes it to be, is not a writer. *L'Inex-primable n'existe pas.*' "

It is either Delacroix or Baudelaire who wrote : " The writer who is incapable of saying everything, who takes unawares and without having enough material to give body to an idea, however subtle or strange or unexpected he may suppose it to be, is not a writer." And one has to beware of the sin of allegory, which spoils even Bunyan's prose. For the deepest emotion raised in us by allegory is a very imperfectly satisfied sense of the writer's ingenuity in overcoming a difficulty we should have preferred his not having attempted to overcome.

Then there is the heresy of instruction—*l'hérésie de l'enseignement*—which Poe and Baudelaire and Swin-burne consider ruinous to art. Art for art's sake first of all ; that a poem must be written for the poem's sake simply, from whatever instinct we have derived it ; it matters nothing whether this be inspired by a prescient ecstasy of the beauty beyond the grave, or by some of that loveliness whose very elements apper-tain solely to eternity. Above all, Verlaine's *Pas de couleur, rien que la nuance !*

The old war—not (as some would foolishly have it defined) a war between facts and fancies, reason and romance, poetry and good sense, but simply between

imagination which apprehends the spirit of a thing
and the understanding which dissects the body of a
fact—the strife which can never be decided—was for
Blake the most important question possible.   Poetry
or art based on loyalty to science is exactly as absurd
(and no more) as science guided by art or poetry.
Though, indeed, Blake wrought his *Marriage of Heaven
and Hell* into a form of absolute magnificence, a prose
fantasy full of splendid masculine thought and of a
diabolical or infernal humour, in which hells and
heavens change names and alternate through mutual
annihilations, which emit an illuminating, devouring,
and unquenchable flame, he never actually attained
the incomparable power of condensing vapour into
tangible and malleable form, of helping us to handle
air and measure mist, which is so instantly perceptible
in Balzac's genius, he who was not " a prose Shakespeare " merely, but rather perhaps a Shakespeare in
all but the lyrical faculty.

Even when Baudelaire expresses his horror of life,
of how abject the world has become, how he himself
is supposed to be " une anomalie," his sense of his own
superiority never leaves him.   " Accursed," as I have
said, such abnormally gifted artists are, he declares
his thirst of glory, a diabolical thirst of fame and of
all kinds of enjoyments—in spite of his " awful temperament, all ruse and violence "—and can say : " I
desire to live and to have self-content.   Something
terrible says to me *never*, and some other thing says
to me *try.   Moi-même, le boulevard m'effraye.*"

Baudelaire's tragic sense of his isolation, of his intense misery, of his series of failures, of his unendurable

existence—it was and was not life—in Brussels finds expression in this sentence, dated September, 1865 : " Les gens qui ne sont pas exilés ne savent pas ce que sont les nerfs de ceux sont cloués à l'étranger, sans communications et sans nouvelles." What he says is the inevitable that has no explanation : simply the inevitable that no man can escape. To be exiled from Paris proves to be, practically, his death-stroke. And, in the last letter he ever wrote, March 5, 1866, there is a sense of irony, of vexation, of wounded pride, and in the last " sting in the tail of the honey " he hisses : " There is enough talent in these young writers ; but what absurdities, what exaggerations, and what youthful infatuations ! Curiously, only a few years ago I perceived these imitators whose tendencies alarmed me I know nothing of a more compromising nature than these : as for me, I love nothing more than being alone. But this is not possible for me, *et il paraît que l'école Baudelaire existe.*"

And, to all appearances, it did ; and what really annoyed Baudelaire was the publication of Verlaine's *Poèmes Saturniens* and their praise by Leconte de l'Isle, Banville, and Hugo ; Hugo, whom he had come to hate. It is with irony that he says of Hugo : " Je n'accepterais ni son génie, ni sa fortune, s'il me fallait au même temps posséder ses énormes ridicules."

III

Here are certain chosen confessions of Baudelaire " For my misery I am not made like other men. I am in a state of spiritual revolt ; I feel as if a wheel turns

G

in my head.   To write a letter costs me more time
than in writing a volume.   My desire of travelling re-
turns on me furiously.   When I listen to the tingling
in my ears that causes me such trouble, I can't help
admiring with what diabolical care imaginative men
amuse themselves in multiplying their embarrass-
ments.   One of my chief preoccupations is to get the
Manager of the Théâtre Porte-Saint-Martin to take
back an actress execrated by his own wife—despite
another actress who is employed in the theatre."   It
is amusing to note that the same desire takes hold of
Gautier, who writes to Arsène Houssaye, the Director
of the Comédie-Française, imploring him to take back
a certain Louise if there is a place vacant for her.

" I can't sleep much now," writes Baudelaire, " as I
am always thinking.   *Quand je dis que je dormirai demain matin, vous devinerez de quel sommeil je veux
parler.*"   This certainly makes me wonder what sort
of sodden sleep he means.   Probably the kind of sleep
he refers to in his Epilogue to the *Poèmes en Prose*,
addressed to Paris :

> " Whether thou sleep, with heavy vapours full,
> Sodden with day, or, new apparelled, stand
> In gold-laced veils of evening beautiful,
>
> I love thee, infamous city ! Harlots and
> Hunted have pleasures of their own to give,
> The vulgar herd can never understand."

The question comes here : How much does Baudelaire give of himself in his letters ?   Some of his inner,
some of his outer life ; but, for the most part, " in
tragic hints."   Yet in the whole of his letters he never

gives one what Meredith does in *Modern Love*, which, published in 1862, remains his masterpiece, and it will always remain, beside certain things of Donne and of Browning, an astonishing feat in the vivisection of the heart in verse. It is packed with imagination, but with imagination of so nakedly human a kind that there is hardly an ornament, hardly an image, in the verse : it is like scraps of broken—of heart-broken—talk, overheard and jotted down at random. These cruel and self-torturing lovers have no illusions, and their tragic hints are like a fine, pained mockery of love itself as they struggle open-eyed against the blindness of passion. The poem laughs while it cries, with a double-mindedness more constant than that of Heine ; with, at times, an acuteness of sensation carried to the point of agony at which Othello sweats words like these :

> " O thou Weed
> Who art so lovely fair, and smell'st so sweet
> That the sense aches at thee, would thou had'st ne'er been
>   born."

Another question arises : How can a man who wrote his letters in a *café*, anywhere, do more than jot down whatever came into his head ? Has he ever given an account of one day in his life—eventful or uneventful ? You might as well try to count the seconds of your watch as try to write for yourself your sensations during one day. What seems terrible is the rapidity of our thoughts : yet, fortunately, one is not always thinking. " Books think for me ; I don't think," says Lamb in one of his paradoxes. There is not much thought in his prose : imagination, humour,

salt and sting, tragical emotions, and, on the whole,
not quite normal. How can any man of genius be
entirely normal ?

The most wonderful letters ever written are Lamb's.
Yet, as in Balzac's, in Baudelaire's, in Browning's, so
few of Lamb's letters, those works of nature, and
almost more wonderful than works of art, are to be
taken on oath. Those elaborate lies, which ramify
through them into patterns of sober-seeming truth,
are in anticipation, and were of the nature of a pre-
liminary practice for the innocent and avowed fiction
of the essays. What began in mischief ends in art.

The life of Baudelaire, like the lives of Balzac and
of Villiers and of Verlaine, was one long labour, in
which time, money, and circumstances were all against
him. "Sometimes," Balzac cries, "it seems to me
that my brain is on fire. I shall die in the trenches of
the intellect." It is his genius, his imagination, that
are on fire, not so much as his sleepless brain. This
certainly Baudelaire never felt. Yet, in one sentence
written in 1861, I find an agony not unlike Balzac's,
but more material, more morbid : " La plupart des
temps je me dis : si je vis, je vivrai toujours de même,
en damné, et quand la mort naturelle viendra, je serai
vieux, usé, passé de mode, criblé de dettes ; ajoute à
cela que je trouve souvent qu'on ne me rend pas
justice, et que je vois que tout réussit à souhait pour
les sots." This, with his perpetual nervous terrors,
his hallucinations, his drugs, his miseries, his women,
his wine, his good and bad nights, his sense of poisonous people, his disorders, his excitability, his imagination that rarely leaves him, his inspiration that often

varies, his phrase, after a certain despair : " Je me suis précipité dans le travail : alors j'ai reconnu que je n'avais perdu aucune faculté ; " his discouragements, his sudden rages, not only against fame, but when he just refrains from hitting a man's face with his stick ; after all this, and after much more than this, I have to take his word when he says—not thinking of these impediments in his way—" What poets ought to do is to know how to escape from themselves."

In 1861 he writes : " As my literary situation is more than good, I can do all I want, I can get all my books printed ; yet, as I have the misfortune in possessing a kind of unpopular spirit, I shall not make much money, but I shall leave a great fame behind me—provided I have the courage to live." " Provided ! " That word sounds a note of nervous distress. He continues : " I have made a certain amount of money ; if I had not had so many debts, *and if I had had more fortune, I might have been rich.*" The last five words he writes in small capitals. And this lamentable refrain is part of his obsession ; wondering, as we all do, why we have never been rich. Then comes this curious statement : " What exasperates me is when I think of what I have received this year ; it is enormous ; certainly I have lived on this money like a ferocious beast ; and yet how often I spend much less than that in sheer waste ! "

VIII

IN 1861 Poulet-Malassis showed Baudelaire the manuscript of *Les Martyrs Ridicules* of Léon Cladel, who was so excited as he read it, so intrigued by his antithetical constructions and by the mere singularity of the title, and so amazed by this writer's audacity, that he made his acquaintance, went over his proofs, and helped to teach him the craft of letters. So, in his sombre and tragic and passionate and feverish novels, we see the inevitable growth out of the hard soil of Quercy, and out of the fertilizing contact of Paris and Baudelaire, of this whole literature, so filled with excitement, so nervous, so voluminous and vehement, in whose pages speech is always out of breath. And one finds splendid variations in his stories of peasants and wrestlers and thieves and prostitutes : something at once epic and morbid.

Baudelaire, in his preface, points out the solemn sadness and the grim irony with which Cladel relates deplorably comic facts ; the fury with which he insists on painting his strange characters ; the fantastic fashion in which he handles sin with the intense curiosity of a casuist, analysing evil and its inevitable consequences. He notes " la puissance sinistrement caricatural de Cladel." But it is in these two sentences that he sums up, supremely, the beginning and the end of realistic and imaginative art. " The Poet,

Peint et Gravé par Manet. 1865   Imp. A. Salmon.

under his mask, still lets himself be seen. But the supremacy of art had consisted in remaining glacial and hermetically sealed, and in leaving to the reader all the merit of indignation. (*Le poète, sous son masque, se laisse encore voir. Le suprême de l'art eût consisté à rester glacial et fermé, et à laisser au lecteur tout le mérite de l'indignation.*)"

Certain of these pages are ironical and sinister and cynical ; as, for instance, in this sentence : " Quant aux insectes amoreux, je ne crois pas que les figures de rhétorique dont ils se servent pour gémir leurs passions soient mesquines ; toutes les mansardes entendant tous les soirs des tirades tragiques dont la Comédie Française ne pourra jamais bénéficier." And it is in regard to this that I give certain details of an anecdote related by Cladel of Baudelaire, which refers to the fatal year when he left Paris for Brussels.

Both often went to the Café de la Belle-Poule ; and, one night, when Cladel was waiting for Baudelaire, a very beautiful woman seated opposite him asked him to present her to Baudelaire. He laughed and they waited, and Baudelaire was presented, who, after giving them the usual drinks, at the end of an hour went away. This went on for a whole month ; when Baudelaire, after her incessant assiduities to him, brought her home with him, Cladel also. They talk. The woman becomes lascivious. Baudelaire answers that he has a passion for beautiful forms and does not wish to expose himself to a deception. She undresses slowly. She is magnificent, and her tresses are so long that, with leaning over a little, she could put her naked feet on the ends of them. She assumes, being probably aware of it, the exact pose of Mademoiselle de Maupin when she stands naked before d'Albert. Cladel goes out. He has not quite closed the door when he hears Baudelaire, prematurely old and worn out, say : " Rhabille-toi." Still vital, he has no more the abstract heat of rapture of the passionate lover in Gautier's famous self-confessions ; for, in that wonderful book, there is nothing besides a delicately depraved imagination and an extreme ecstasy over the flesh and the senses. And he also realized, as Baudelaire did not always, that the beauty of life was what he wanted, and not the body, that frail and perishable thing, that has to be pitied, that so many desire to perpetuate.

Yet never in Baudelaire, as in Gautier, did the five senses become articulate, as if they were made specially for him ; for he speaks for them with a dreadful unconcern. All his words are—never Baudelaire's—in love with matter, and they enjoy their lust and have no recollection. Yet neither were absolutely content with the beauty of a woman's body : for the body must finally dwindle and expand to some ignoble physical condition, and on certain women's necks wrinkles will crawl, and the fire in one's blood sometimes loses some of its heat ; only, one wants to perpetuate the beauty of life itself, imperishable at least in its recurrence.

In his preface Baudelaire compares Murger with Musset, both Bohemian classics, only one spoke of Bohemia with a bitter bantering, and the poet, when he was not in his noble moods, had crises of fatuity. " All this evil society, with its vile habits, its adven-

turous morals, was painted by the vivid pencil-strokes
of Murger ; only he jested in his relations of miserable
things." Yes, Murger is a veracious historian ; believe
him, if you do not know or have forgotten, that such
are the annals of Bohemia. There, people laugh just
so lightly and sincerely, weep and laugh just as freely,
are really hungry, really have their ambitions, and at
times die of all these maladies. It is the gayest and
most melancholy country in the world. To have lived
there too long, is to find all the rest of the world in
exile. But if you have been there or not, read Murger's
pages ; there, perhaps, you will see more of the country
than anything less than a lifetime spent in it will show
you.

IX

IN April, 1864, Baudelaire left Paris for Brussels, where he stayed in the Hôtel du Grand-Miroir, rue de la Montagne. Before then his nerves had begun to torment him ; they played tricks with his very system ; he wrote very little prose and no verse. It was with a kind of desperate obstination—a more than desperate obstinacy—that he strove to prevent himself from giving way to his pessimistic conceptions of life, to his morbid over-sensibility that ached as his flesh ached. Unsatiated, unsatisfied, for once in his existence irresolute in regard to what he wanted to do, watching himself with an almost casuistical casuistry, alone and yet not alone in the streets of Paris, he wandered, a *noctambule*, night after night, sombre and sinister. So a ghost self-obsessed might wander in desolate cities seeing ever before him the Angel of Destruction.

Did he then know that he was becoming more and more abnormal ? This I ignore. This, I suppose, he alone knew ; and hated too much knowledge of his precarious condition. He was veritably more alone than ever, before he plunged—as one who might see shipwreck before him—into that gulf that is no gulf, that extends not between hell and heaven, but that one names Brussels.

Still he frequented his favourite haunts, the Moulin-Rouge, the Casino de la rue Cadet, and other cabarets.

Mon cher ami ! Je suis
jusqu'à ce jour de vous
avoir raconté tout ce que
vous savez ; Today ! j'ai vous
m'avez pris encore Vie Gautier
au Mon[...] et ou[...] au[...]
s'[...] mes de[...] de Jos égales
la haïr contre moi. Car
j'ai [...] figaro. Je [...] en
[...] a jour je il y a accum de
la absorba Joujs à par
d'[...] !

Ch. Baudelaire

M. Charles
Asselineau
———

He saw then, as I saw many years afterwards, pass
some of his Flowers of Evil—some who knew him and
had read his verses, most of whom he ignored—
macabre, with hectic cheeks and tortured eyes and
painted faces ; these strange nocturnal birds of passage
that flit to and fro, the dancers and the hired women ;
always—so Latin an attitude of their traditional trade !
—with enquiring and sidelong glances at men and at
women.

I can see him now, as I write, sit in certain corners
of the Moulin-Rouge—as I did—drinking strange
drinks and smoking cigarettes ; hearing with all his
old sensuality that adorable and cynical and perverse
and fascinating *Valse des Roses* of Olivier Métra : a
maddening music to the soundless sound of the mad
dances of the *Chahut*—danced by dancers of both
sexes, ambiguous and exotic and neurotic—that, as
the avid circle forms hastily around them, set their
fevers into our fevers, their nerves into our nerves.

It was in May, 1892, that, having crossed the streets
of Paris from the hotel where I was staying, the Hôtel
Corneille, in the Latin Quarter (made famous by
Balzac in his superb story, *Z. Marcas*), I found myself
in Le Jardin de Paris, where I saw for the first time
La Mélinite. She danced in a quadrille : young and
girlish, the more provocative because she played as a
prude, with an assumed modesty ; *décolletée* nearly to
the waist, in the Oriental fashion. She had long, black
curls around her face ; and had about her a depraved
virginity.

And she caused in me, even then, a curious sense of
depravity that perhaps comes into the verses I wrote

on her. There, certainly, on the night of May 22nd,
danced in her feverish, her perverse, her enigmatical
beauty, La Mélinite, to her own image in the mirror :

> " A shadow smiling
> Back to a shadow in the night,"

as she cadenced Olivier Métra's *Valse des Roses*.

It is a fact of curious interest that in 1864 Poulet-
Malassis was obliged to leave Paris—on account of his
misfortunes as a publisher, in regard to money, and for
various other reasons—and to exile himself in Brussels :
still more curious that Baudelaire—drawn, perhaps, by
some kind of affinity in their natures—followed him
sooner than he had intended to go. Malassis lived in
rue de Mercedes, 35 *bis*, Faubourg d'Ixilles. In those
years both saw a great deal of the famous, perverse,
macabre Félicien Rops.

Malassis, naturally, was obliged, in his expedients
for living as he used to live, to publish privately printed
obscene books ; some no more than erotic. As Baudelaire hated, with his Parisian refinement, that kind of
certainly objectionable literature, on May 4th, 1865,
he writes to Sainte-Beuve : " As for Malassis, his
terrible affair arrives on the 12th. He believes he will
be condemned for five years. What there is grave in
this is that that closes France for him for five years.
But that cuts him for a time from his ways of living.
I see in it no great evil. As for me, who am no fool,
I have never possessed one of these idiotic books, even
printed in fine characters and with fine engravings."
As a matter of fact, Malassis was condemned in May,
1866, to one year's imprisonment for having privately

printed *Les Amies* of Paul Verlaine—a book of sonnets, attributed to an imaginary Pablo de Herlaguez.

Baudelaire, as I have said, had many reasons for going to Brussels. Among these was his urgent desire of finding a publisher to print his collected works— having failed to find any publisher for them. Another was that of giving lectures—a thing he was not made for—and for two other reasons : one of making immediate money, one of adding to his fame as a writer. Then, to write a book on Belgium.

He writes to Manet (who has written to him : " Do return to Paris ! No happiness can come to you while you live in that damned country ! ") : " As for finishing here *Pauvre Belgique*, I am incapable of it : I am near on dead. I have quite a lot of *Poèmes en Prose* to get printed in magazines. I can do no more than that. *Je souffre d'un mal qui je n'ai pas, comme j'étais gamin, et que je vivais au bout du monde.*"

His book was to have been humorous, mocking, and serious — his final separation from modern stupidity. " People may understand me, perhaps, then." " Nothing," he confesses, " can console me in my detestable misery, in my humiliating situation, nor especially in my vices."

In February, 1865, he writes : " As for my present state, it is an absolute abdication of the will. (*C'est une parfaite abdication de la volonté.*)" What reason, I wonder, was there for him to " abdicate " the one element in our natures by which we live at our greatest, the very root of our passions (as Balzac said), " nervous fluids and that unknown substance which, in default of another term, we must call the will ? " Man has a

given quality of energy ; each man a different quality :
how will he spend it ? That is Balzac's invariable
question. All these qualities were always in Baudelaire.

Had he finally, after so many years in which his
energy was supreme, lost some of his energy, struggling,
as he seems to do, against insuperable difficulties that
beset him on either side, like thieves that follow men
in the dark with the intention of stabbing you in the
back ? Does he then try to conjecture what next year
might bring him of good or of evil ? He has lived his
life after his own will : what shall the end be ? He
dares neither look backward nor forward. It might be
that he feels the earth crumbling under his feet ; for
how many artists have had that fear—the fear that
the earth under their feet may no longer be solid ?
There is another step for him to take, a step that
frightens him ; might it not be into another more pain-
ful kind of oblivion ? Has something of the man gone
out of him: that is to say, the power to live for himself ?

In the summer of 1865 Baudelaire spent several days
in Paris, seeing Banville and other friends of his. They
found him unchanged ; his eyes clear ; his voice
musical ; he talked as wonderfully as ever. They used
all their logic to persuade him to remain in Paris. He
refused, even after Gautier had said to him : " You
are astonishing : can one conceive your mania of
eternalizing yourself in a land where one is only bored
to extinction ? " He laughed ; promised to return :
he never did ; it was the last day when his friends
possessed him entirely.

In his years of exile he printed Poe's *Histoires
Grotesques et Sérieuses* (1864) ; *Les Nouvelles Fleurs du*

Mal in *La Parnasse Contemporaine* (1866). In 1865 Poulet-Malassis printed *Les Epaves de Charles Baudelaire*. Avec une eau-forte de Félicien Rops. Amsterdam. A l'enseigne du Coq. 1865. 165 pages.

" Avertissement de l'Editeur.

" Ce recueil est composé de morceaux poétiques, pour la plupart condamnés ou inédits, auxquels M. Charles Baudelaire n'a pas cru devoir faire place dans l'édition définitive des *Fleurs du Mal*.

" Cela explique son title.

" M. Charles Baudelaire a fait don, sans réserve, de ces poëmes, à un ami qui juge à propos de les publier, parce qu'il se flatte de les goûter, et qu'il est à un âge où l'on aime encore à faire partager ses sentiments à des amis auxquels on prête ses vertus.

" L'auteurs sera avisé de cette publication en même temps que les deux cents soixantes lectures probables qui figurent—à peu près—pour son éditeur bénévole, le public littéraire en France, depuis que les bêtes y ont décidément usurpé la parole sur les hommes."

I have before me two copies of this rare edition, printed on yellow Holland paper ; one numbered 100, the other 194. The second has inscribed in ink : *A Monsieur Rossetti pour remplir les intentions de l'auteur avec les civilités de l'éditeur A. P. Malassis.* This was sent on the part of Baudelaire to Dante Gabriel Rossetti. It is superbly bound in a kind of red-purple thick leather binding, with pale gold squares, in the form of the frame of a picture ; done, certainly, with great taste.

On January 3, 1865, Baudelaire writes a letter to his mother ; a letter that pains one as one reads it :

so resigned he seems to be, yet never in his life less resigned to his fate. He fears that God might deprive him of even happiness ; that it is more difficult to think than to write a book ; that if only he were certain of having five or six years before him he might execute all that remained for him to do ; that he has the fixed idea of death ; that he has suffered so much already that he believes many things may be forgiven him (sins of concupiscence, sins of conscience, sins one never forgets) as he has been punished so much.

I pass from this to the beginning of March, 1866. He stays with Rops at Namur, where (certainly by bad luck) he enters again l'Eglise Saint-Loup, which he had spoken of as " this sinister marvel in the interior of a catafalque—terrible and delicious—broidered with gold, red, and silver." As he admires these richly sculptured confessionals, as he speaks with Rops and Malassis, he stumbles, taken by a kind of dizziness in the head, and sits down on a step in the church. They lift him up ; he feigns not to be frightened, says that his foot had slipped accidentally. Next day he shows signs of a nervous trouble, not a mental one ; asking them in the train to Brussels to have the window opened ; it is open. That is the first sign of his loss of speech, and the last letter that he ever wrote (dated March 30th, 1866), ends : *Je ne puis pas bouger.* It is strange to set beside this Balzac's last words, that end a letter written June 20th, 1856 : *Je ne puis ni lire ni écrire.* It is written to Théophile Gautier.

Swinburne, having heard the fatal news in regard to Baudelaire, added to his book on Blake these magnificent words : as pure, as fervent a tribute to the

memory of a fellow-artist as Baudelaire might have
wished to have been written on himself, as Swinburne
might have desired to have been written on himself :
" I heard that a mortal illness had indeed stricken the
illustrious poet, the faultless critic, the fearless artist ;
that no more of fervent yet of perfect verse, no more
of subtle yet of sensitive comment, will be granted us
at the hands of Charles Baudelaire. We may see again
as various a power as was his, may feel again as fiery
a sympathy, may hear again as tragic a manner of
revelation, as sad a whisper of knowledge, as mysterious a music of emotion ; we shall never find so keen,
so delicate, so deep an unison of sense and spirit.
What verse he could make, how he loved all fair and
felt all strange things, with what infallible taste he
knew at once the limit and the licence of his art, all
may see at a glance. He could give beauty to the
form, expression to the feeling, most horrible and most
obscure to the senses or souls of lesser men. The chances
of things parted us once and again ; the admiration of
some years, at least in part expressed, brought him
near to me by way of written or transmitted word ;
let it be an excuse for the insertion of this note, and
for a desire, if so it must be, to repeat for once the
immortal words which too often return upon our lips :

Atque in perpetuum, frater, ave atque vale ! "

And I, who have transcribed these words, have
before me a book that Swinburne showed me, that he
had richly bound in Paris, and that I bought at the
sale of his library on June 19th : *Richard Wagner et
Tannhäuser à Paris.* Par Charles Baudelaire. Paris,

H

1861 ; with, written in pencil, on the page before the title-page, these words :

> *"A Mr. Algernon C. Swinburne.   Bon Souvenir et mille Remerciements.   C. B."*

From April 9, 1866, to August 31, 1867, Baudelaire endures the slow tortures of a body and a soul condemned to go on living ; living, what else can it be called, than a kind of living death ? To remain, in most senses, himself ; to be, as always, Charles Baudelaire ; to have in his mind one desire, the desire, the vain desire, of recovery ; to be unable to utter one word ; to think, to sleep, to conceive imaginary projects, for his near future, for his verse, for his prose : to walk, to eat, to drink ; to be terribly conscious of his dolorous situation ; to be, as ever, anxious for a new edition of *Les Fleurs du Mal ;* to mark a date in an almanac, counting three months, when he imagined he would be in a state to superintend the impression of his final edition ; to have finally given up all hope, all illusion ; to have gazed out of his wonderful eyes, at his friend's faces, eyes shadowed by an expression of infinite sadness, eyes that endured his last tragedy : that is how Baudelaire survived himself to the end.

He died on Saturday, August 31, 1867, at eleven o'clock in the morning, at the age of forty-six and four months. So died, simply and without any trace of suffering, this man of genius. Had he been thoroughly understood by the age in which he lived ? Blake, who said the final truth on this question : " The ages are all equal ; but genius is always above the ages : " was not understood in his age.

BIBLIOGRAPHY AND NOTES

I

1 *Salon de* 1845. Par Baudelaire-Dufays. Paris, Jules Labitte, 1845. 72 pp.

2 *Salon de* 1846. Par Baudelaire-Dufays. Paris, Michel Lévy, 1846. 132 pp.

3. *Histoires Extraordinaires.* Par Edgar Poe. Traduction de Charles Baudelaire. Paris, Michel Lévy, 1856.
   1. Edgar Poe, La Vie et Ses Œuvres, pp. vii–xxxi. 2. Translations, 323 pp.

4. *Nouvelles Histoires Extraordinaires.* Par Edgar Poe. Traduction de Charles Baudelaire. Michel Lévy, 1857.
   1. Notes nouvelles sur Edgar Poe, pp. v–xxiv. 2. Translations, 288 pp.

5. *Les Fleurs du Mal.* Par Charles Baudelaire. Paris, Poulet-Malassis et de Broise, 4 rue de Buci, 1857. 252 pp.
   1. Dédicace. 2. Au Lecteur.
   SPLEEN ET IDÉAL.—1. Bénédiction. 2. Le Soleil. 3. Elévation. 4. Correspondances. 5. *J'aime le souvenir de ces époques nues.* 6. Les Phares. 7. La Muse Malade. 8. La Muse Venale. 9. Le Mauvais Moine. 10. L'Ennemi. 11. Le Guignon. 12. La Vie Intérieure. 13. Bohémiens en Voyage. 14. L'Homme et la Mer. 15. Don Juan aux Enfers. 16. Châtiment de l'Orgueil. 17. La Beauté. 18. L'Idéal. 19. La Géante. 20. Les Bijoux. 21. Parfum Exotique. 22. *Je t'adore à l'égal de la voûte nocturne.* 23. *Tu mettre l'univers entier dans ta ruelle.* 24. Sed non Satiata. 25. *Avec ses vêtements ondoyants et nacrés.* 26. Le Serpent qui danse. 27. La Charogne. 28. *De Profundis Clamavis.* 29. Le Vampire. 30. Le Léthé. 31. *Une nuit que j'étais près d'une affreuse Juive.* 32. Remords posthume. 33. Le Chat. 34. Le Balcon. 35. *Je te donne ces vers afin que si mon nom.* 36. Tout entière. 37. *Que diras-tu ce soir, pauvre âme solitaire.* 38. Le Flambeau vivant. 39. A Celle qui est trop gaie. 40. Réversibilité. 41. Confession. 42. L'Aube Spirituelle. 43. Harmonie du Soir. 44. Le Flacon. 45. Le Poison. 46. Ciel brouillé. 47. Le Chat. 48. Le Beau Navire. 49. L'Invitation au Voyage. 50. L'Irréparable. 51. Causerie. 52. L'Héautontimouroménos. 53. Franciscae meae laudes. 54. A une Dame Créole. 55. Moesta et Errabunda. 56. Les Chats. 57. Les Hiboux. 58. La Cloche Fêlée. 59. Spleen. 60. Spleen. 61. Spleen. 62. Spleen. 63. Brumes et Pluies. 64. L'Irrémédiable. 65. A une Mendiante rousse. 66. Le Jeu. 67. Le Crépuscule du Soir. 68. Le Crépuscule du Matin. 69. *Le servante au grand cœur dont vous étiez jaloux.* 70. *Je n'ai pas oublié, voisine de la ville.* 71. Le Tonneau de la Haine. 72. Le Revenant. 73. Le Mort Joyeux. 74. Sépulture. 75. Tristesses de la Lune. 76. La Musique. 77. La Pipe.
   FLEURS DU MAL.—78. La Destruction. 79. Une Martyr. 80. Lesbos. 81. Femmes damnées (Delphine et Hippolyte). 82. Femmes damnées. 83. Les Deux bonnes Sœurs. 84. La Fontaine de Sang. 85. Allégorie. 86. La Beatrice. 87. Les Metamorphoses du Vampire. 88. Un Voyage à Cythère. 89. L'Amour et le Crâne.

RÉVOLTE.—90. Le Reniement de Saint Pierre. 91. Abel et Caïn. 92. Les Litanies de Satan.

LE VIN.—93. L'âme du Vin. 94. Le Vin des Chiffonniers. 95. Le Vin de l'Assassin. 96. Le Vin du Solitaire. 97. Le Vin des Amants.

LA MORT.—98. La Mort des amants. 99. La Mort des Pauvres. 100. La Mort des Artistes.

6. *Aventures d'Arthur Gordon Pym.* Par Edgar Poe. Traduction de Charles Baudelaire. Paris, Michel Lévy, 1858. 200 pp.

7. *Théophile Gautier.* Par Charles Baudelaire. Notice Littéraire précédée d'une lettre de Victor Hugo. Paris, Poulet-Malassis et de Broise, 9 rue des Beaux-Arts, 1859.

    1. A M. Charles Baudelaire de Victor Hugo, pp. i, iii. 2. Théophile Gautier, 68 pp.

8. *Les Paradis Artificiels : Opium et Haschisch.* Par Charles Baudelaire. Paris, Poulet-Malassis et de Broise, 9 rue des Beaux-Arts, 1860.

    1. Dédicace à J. G. F., pp. i–iv. 2. Le Poème du Haschisch, pp. 1–108. 3. Un Mangeur d'Opium, pp. 109–304.

On the back of the cover is this announcement :

" Sous Presse, du même auteur : *Réflexions sur quelques-uns, de mes Contemporains ;* un volume contenant : Edgar Poe, Théophile Gautier, Pierre Dupont, Richard Wagner, Auguste Barbier, Leconte de Lisle, Hégisippe Moreau, Pétrus Borel, Marceline Desbordes-Valmore, Gustave le Vavasseur, Gustave Flaubert, Philibert Rouvière ; la famille des *Dandies*, ou Chateaubriand, de Custine, Paul de Molinès, and Barbey d'Aurévilly."

This volume appeared in part in *L'Art Romantique* (1868) ; several of these essays were never written, such as the one on Barbey d'Aurévilly.

Séconde Edition, 1861.

9. *Les Fleurs du Mal* de Charles Baudelaire.

Séconde Edition augmentée de trente-cinq poëmes nouveaux et orné d'un Portrait de l'Auteur dessiné et gravé par Bracquemond. Paris, Poulet-Malassis et de Broise, Editeurs, 97 rue de Richelieu et Passage Mirès, 1861. 319 pp.

    1. L'Albatros. 2. Le Masque. Statue Allégorique dans le goût de la Renaissance. 3. Hymne à la Beauté. 4. La Chevelure. 5. Duellum. 6. Le Possédé. 7. Un Fantôme : (1) Les Ténèbres. (2) Le Parfum. (3) Le Cadre. (4) Le Portrait. 8. Sempre Eadem. 9. Chant d'Automne. 10. A Une Madone. Ex-Voto dans le goût Espagnol. 11. Chanson d'Après-Midi. 12. Sisine. 13. Sonnet d'Automne. 14. Une Gravure Fantastique. 15. Obsession. 16. Le Goût du Néant. 17. Alchimie de la Douleur. 18. Horreur Sympathique. 19. L'Horloge. 20. Un Paysage. 21 Le Cynge. 22. Les Sept Vieillards. 23. Les Petites Vieilles. 24. Les Aveugles. 25. A une Passante. 26. Le Squelette Laboureux. 27. Danse Macabre. 28. L'Amour du Mensonge. 29. Rêve Parisien. 30. La Fin de la Journée. 31. Le Rêve d'un Curieux. 32. Le Voyage.

10. *Richard Wagner et Tannhäuser* à Paris. Par Charles Baudelaire. Paris, E. Dentu, Palais-Royale, 13 et 17, Galérie d'Orléans, 1861. 70 pp.

11. *Euréka.* Par Edgar Poe. Traduction par Charles Baudelaire. Paris, Michel Lévy, 1864. 252 pp.

12. *Histoires Grotesques et Sérieuses.* Par Edgar Poe. Traduction par Charles Baudelaire. Paris, Michel Lévy, 1865. 372 pp.

13. *Les Epaves* de Charles Baudelaire. Avec une Eau-forte. Frontispiece de Félicien Rops. Amsterdam, à l'Enseigne du Coq, 1865.

    1. Avertissement de l'Editeur, pp. i–iii.   2. Les Epaves, 163 pp.

14. *Les Epaves* de Charles Baudelaire. Avec une Eau-forte de Félicien Rops. Amsterdam, à l'Enseigne du Coq, 1865. Numero 194.

15. *Les Epaves* de Charles Baudelaire. Avec une Eau-forte de Félicien Rops. Amsterdam, à l'Enseigne du Coq, 1865. Numero 100.

> *A Monsieur Rossetti pour remplir les intentions de l'auteur, avec les civilités de l'Editeur. A. P. Malassis.*

II

Edition Définitive des Œuvres de Charles Baudelaire. Paris, Michel Lévy et Frères, Libraires Editeurs, rue Vivienne, 2 *bis*, et Boulevard des Italiens, 15. A la Librairie Nouvelle, 1868–1869.

Volume I. LES FLEURS DU MAL. 414 pp.

Volume II. CURIOSITÉS ESTHÉTIQUES. 440 pp.

    1. Salon de 1845. 2. Salon de 1846. 3. Le Musée Classique du Bazar Bonne Nouvelle (1846). 4. Exposition Universale de 1855. Beaux Arts (1855). 5. Salon de 1850. 6. De l'Essence du Rire, et généralement du Comique dans les Arts Plastiques. 7. Quelques Caricaturistes Français : Carle Vernet. Pigal. Charlet. Daumier. Henri Monnier. Grandville. Gavarni. Trimolet. Traviès. Jacque (1857). 8. Quelques Caricaturistes Étrangers : Hogarth. Cruikshank. Goya. Pinelli. Breughel (1857).

Volume III. L'ART ROMANTIQUE.

    1. L'Œuvre et la Vie d'Eugène Delacroix (1862). 2. Peintures murales d'Eugène Delacroix à Saint-Sulpice (1861). 3. Le Peintre de la Vie Moderne. Constantin Guys (1862). 4. Peintres et Aqua-fortistes (1862). 5. Vente de le Collection de M. E. Piot (1864). 6. L'Art Philosophique. 7. Morale des Joujou (1854). 8. Théophile Gautier (1859–1861–1862). 9. Pierre Dupont (1852–1861–1862). 10. Richard Wagner et Tannhäuser à Paris. Encore

6. CHARLES BAUDELAIRE (1821–1867). Par Féli Gautier. Orné de 26 Portraits différents du Poète et de 28 Gravures et Reproductions. Bruxelles, E. Deman, 1904. Tirage à 150 Exemplaires numérotés. Exemplaire No. 74.

7. VERSIFICATION ET METRIQUE DE BAUDELAIRE. Par Albert Cassagne. Paris, Hachette, 1906.

8. LETTRES (1841–1866) DE CHARLES BAUDELAIRE. Paris, Mercure de France, 1908.

9. ŒUVRES POSTHUMES DE CHARLES BAUDELAIRE. Paris, Mercure de France, 1908.

10. LE CARNET DE CHARLES BAUDELAIRE. 1911.

Publié avec une Introduction et des Notes par Féli Gautier et orné d'un dessin inédit de Baudelaire. Paris, J. Chevrel, Libraire 29 rue de Seine. Cette plaquette non mise dans le commerce à été tirée à cent exemplaires sur papier velin d'arches. Numéro 27.

This *petit carnot vert*, which contains seven quires of twenty-four pages—the last two have been torn out—was used by Baudelaire for noting down certain private details, details of almost every kind, which he began in 1861 and ended in 1864. There are lists of his debts, of his friends, of his enemies, of his projects, of his proofs, of his books, of his articles, of the people he has to see and to write to, of the etchings and drawings he buys or intends to buy, of the money he owes and of the money he is in the utmost need of. On one page is the original text of his dedication of the " Poems on Prose." On one page he reckons forty days in which to execute some of his translations, his prose, and his poems. On another page he gives a list of his hatreds, underlining *Vilainies, Canailles ;* then his plans for short stories and dramas. These notes are of importance. " Faire en un an 2 vols. *de Nouvelles* et *Mon Cœur mis à nu.*" " *Tous les jours cinq poèmes et autre chose.*" Then this sinister note : " Pour faire du neuf, quitter Paris, ou je me meurs." After this come long lists of the women he frequents and of their addresses, such as 29 rue Neuve Bréda, 36 rue Cigalle. After this comes Swinburne's verses, with the list of the few friends he possesses : Villiers, Noriac, Manet, Malassis, his mother ; together with Louise, Gabrielle, and Judith.

11. LETTRES INÉDITÉS A SA MÈRE (1833–1866). Par Charles Baudelaire. Louis Conard, Libraire Editeur, 6 Place de la Madeleine, Paris, 1918. Numéro 182.

12. JOURNEAUX INTIMES DE CHARLES BAUDELAIRE : TEXTE INTEGRAL. Paris, Georges Crès, 21 rue Hautefeuille, 1919.

This edition is founded on the original manuscripts of Baudelaire, now in the possession of Gabriel Thomas.

FUSÉES. A manuscript of fifteen pages, containing twenty-two sections numbered in red ink ; the pagination is also in red ink. The notes have, often enough, the aspect of mere fragments, scrawled angrily. One of them, numbered 53, and two paragraphs of another (the note 17 : *Tantôt il lui demandait ; Minette*) are written in pencil ; note 12 is written in blue ink. Certain phrases in the text are used twice over.

MON CŒUR MIS À NU. A manuscript of 91 pages, containing 197 articles numbered in red ink ; the pagination used in the same way as in the other. Every note is preceded with the autograph mention : *Mon Cœur mis à nu.* The text is written rapidly ; the notes numbered 26, 31, 44, 48, 51, 54, 60, 68, 69, 72, 75 (the last three in italics), 80 are written with a black pencil, the note 62 with a black pencil on blue paper, and the note 83 written with a red pencil.

çaise " instead of " *au parfait magicien ès-lettres françaises,*" which he corrected in the edition of 1861.

On July 11, 1857, he writes to Malassis : " Quick, hide the edition, the whole edition. I have saved fifty here. The mistake was in having sent a copy to *Le Figaro !* As the edition was sold out in three weeks we may have the glory of a trial, from which we can easily escape." The trial came ; he was obliged to suppress six poems (supposed to contain " obscene and immoral passages "). Baudelaire never ceased to protest against the infamy of this trial. A copy of the second edition (not nearly so well printed as the first) is before me : LES FLEURS DU MAL. || Par Charles Baudelaire. || Seconde Edition. || Augmentée de trente-cinq poèmes nouveaux || et ornée d'un portrait de l'auteur dessiné et gravé par Bracquemont. || Paris : || Poulet-Malassis et de Broise. || Editeurs. || 97. Rue de Richelieu, et Beaux-Arts, 56. || 1861. || Tout droits reservés. || Paris : Imp. Simon Raçon et Comp. || Rue d'Erfurth.

In comparing the text of 1857 with that of 1861 I find several revisions of certain verses, not always, I think, for the best. For instance, in the *Préface,* the first edition is as follows :

> " Dans nos cervaux malsains, comme un million d'helminthes,
> Grouille, chante et ripaille un peuple de Démons."

He changes this into " verre fourmillant ; " " dans nos cervaux ribote." On page 22, he writes :

> " Sent un froid ténébreux envelopper son âme
> A l'aspect du tableau plein d'épouvantement
> Des monstruosités, que voile un vêtement :
> Des visages masqués et plus laids que des masques."

In the later text he puts a full stop after " épouvantement," and continues :

> " O monstruosités pleurant leur vêtement !
> O ridicules troncs ! torses dignes des masques."

This reading seems to me infinitely inferior to the reading of the first version.

Again, there are certain other changes, even less happy, such as " *quadrature* " into " *nature,*" " *divin élixir* " into " *comme un élixir,*" "*Mon âme se balançait comme un ange joyeux,*" into "*Mon cœur, comme un oiseau, voltigeant tout joyeux.*" Baudelaire, in sending a copy of *Les Fleurs du Mal* (1861) to Alfred de Vigny, wrote that he had marked the new poems in pencil in the list at the end of the book. In my copy—1857—he has marked, with infinite delicacy, in pencil, only three poems : " Lesbos," " Femmes Dammées," " Les Metamorphoses du Vampire." He underlines, in " Une Charogne," these words in the text : " *charogne lubrique, cynique, ventre, d'exhalaisons.*" At one side of the prose note on " Franciscae meae laudes " he has made, on the margin, a number of arrows.

II

In *Le Corsaire-Satan*, January, 1848, Baudelaire reviewed three books of short stories by Champfleury. On the first, *Chien-Caillou*, he writes : " One day a quite small, quite simple volume, *Chien-Caillou*, was printed ; the history simply, clearly, crudely related, of a poor engraver, certainly original, but whose poverty was so extreme that he lived on carrots, between a rabbit and a girl of the town ; and he made masterpieces." I have before me this book : " *Chien-Caillou, Fantasies d'Hiver*. Par Champfleury. Paris. A la Librarie Pittoresque de Martinon. Rue du Coq-Saint-Martin, 1847." It is dedicated to Victor Hugo. " I dedicate to you this work, in spite of the fact that I have an absolute horror of dedications—because of the expression *young man* that it leaves in readers' minds. But you have been the first to signalize *Chien-Caillou* to your friends, and your luminous genius has suddenly recognized the reality of the second title : *This is not a Story*."

In the same year came out *La Gâteau des Rois*. Par M. Jules Janin. Ouvrage entièrement inédit. Paris. Librarie d'Amyot, 6 rue de la Paix, 1847. I have my own copy of this edition, bound in pale yellow-paper covers.

On January 26th, 1917, there came to me from Paris an original manuscript, written by Charles Baudelaire on three pages of note-paper, concerning these two books of Champfleury and Jules Janin. Being unfinished, it may have been the beginning of an essay which he never completed. Certainly I find no trace of this prose in any of his printed books. From the brown colour of the ink that he used I think it was written in 1857, as the ink and the handwriting are absolutely the same as in his signed *Fleurs du Mal* sent to Champfleury. There are several revisions and corrections in the text of the MS. that I possess.

At the top of the first page are nearly obliterated the words : *remplacez les blancs*. It begins : " Pour donner immédiatement au lecteur non initié dans les dessous de la littérature, non instruit dans les préliminaires des réputations, une idée première de l'importance littéraire réille de ces petits livres, gros d'esprit, de poésie et d'obser-vations, qu'il sache que le premier d'entre nous, *Chien-Caillou*, Fantasies d'Hiver, fut publié en même temps qu'un petit livre d'un homme très célèbre, qui avait, en même temps que Champfleury, l'idée de ces publications en trimestrielles." It ends : " Où est le cœur ? Où est l'âme, où est la raison ? "

Here is my translation :

" To convey to the reader who has not penetrated into the back-parlours of literature, who has not been instructed in the prelimi-naries of reputations, an immediate idea of the real literary import-ance of these little books, fat in wit, poetry, and observations, it should be stated that the first among them, *Chien-Caillou*, Fantasies d'Hiver, was published at the same time as another small book by a famous man who had, simultaneously with Champfleury, started these quarterly publications.

" Now, for these people whose intelligence, daily applied to the elaboration of books, is hardest to please, Champfleury's work absorbed that of the famous man. All those of whom I speak have known *Le Gâteau des Rois*. Their profession is to know everything. *Le Gâteau des Rois*, a kind of Christmas book, or ' Livre de Noël,' showed above all a clearly asserted pretention to draw from the language, by playing infinite variations on the dictionary, all the effects which a transcendental instrumentalist draws from his chords. Shifting of forces, error of an unballasted mind ! The ideas in this strange book follow each other in haste, dart with the swiftness of sound, leaning at random on infinitely tenuous connections. Their association with one another hangs by a thread according to a method of thought similar to that of people in Bedlam.

" Vast current of involuntary ideas, wild-goose chase, abnegation of will ! This singular feat of dexterity was accomplished by the man you know, whose sole and special faculty consists in not being master of himself, the man of encounters and good fortunes.

" Assuredly there was talent. But what abuse ! What debauchery ! And, besides, what fatigue and what pain !

" No doubt some respect is due or, at least, some grateful compassion, for the tireless writhing of an old dancing girl. But, alas ! worn-out attitudes, weak methods, boresome seductivities !

" The ideas of our man are but old women driven crazy with too much dancing, too much kicking off the ground. *Sustalerunt sœpius pedes*.

" Where is the heart ? Where the soul ? Where reason ? "

Here the manuscript comes to an abrupt end, and one is left to wonder how much more Baudelaire had written ; perhaps only one more page, as he had a peculiar fashion of writing fragments on bits of note-paper. Certainly this prose has the refinement, the satire, the exquisite use of words, the inimitable charm and unerring instinct of a faultless writer. Not only is there his passion for *les danseuses* and for the exotic, but a sinister touch in *l'abdication de la volonté* which recurs finally in a letter written February 8, 1865 ; for, when one imagines himself capable of an absolute abdication of the will, it means that something of the man has gone out of him.

III.　AN ADVENTURE IN IMAGES

It is often said, not without a certain kind of truth, that the likeness is precisely what matters least in a portrait. That is one of the interesting heresies which Whistler did not learn from Velasquez. Because a portrait which is a likeness, and nothing more than a likeness, can often be done by a second-rate artist, by a kind of sympathetic trick, it need not follow that likeness is in itself an unimportant quality in a masterly portrait, nor will it be found that likeness was ever disregarded by the greatest painters. But there are many kinds of likenesses, among which we have to choose, as we have to choose in all art which follows nature, between a realism of outward circumstance and a realism of inner significance. Every individual face has as many different expressions as the soul behind it has moods. When we talk, currently, of a " good likeness," we mean, for the most part, that a single, habitual expression, with which we are familiar, as we are familiar with a frequently worn suit of clothes, has been rendered ; that we see a man as we imagine ourselves ordinarily to see him. But, in the first place, most people see nothing with any sort of precision ; they cannot tell you the position and shape of the ears, or the shape of the cheek-bones, of their most intimate friends. Their mental vision is so feeble that they can call up only a blurred image, a vague compromise between expressions, without any definite form at all. Others have a mental vision so sharp, retentive, yet without selection, that to think of a person is to call up a whole series of precise images, each the image of a particular expression at a particular moment ; the whole series failing to coalesce into one really typical likeness, the likeness of soul or body. Now it is the artist's business to choose among these mental pictures ; better still, to create on paper, or on his canvas, the image which was none of these, but which these helped to make in his own soul.

The Manet portrait of Charles Baudelaire, dated 1862, is exquisite, ironical, subtle, enigmatical, astonishing. He has arrested the head and shoulders of the poet in an instant's vision ; the outlines are definite, clear, severe, and simple. One sees the eager head thrust forward, as if the man were actually walking ; the fine and delicate nose, voluptuously dilated in the nostrils, seems to breathe in vague perfumes ; the mouth, half-seen, has a touch of his malicious irony ; the right eye shines vividly in a fixed glance, those eyes that had the colour of Spanish tobacco. Over the long, waving hair, that seems to be swept backward by the wind, is placed, with unerring skill, at the exact angle, that top-hat that Baudelaire had to have expressly made to fit the size of his head. Around his long neck is just seen the white soft collar of his shirt, with a twisted tie in front. In this picture one sees the inspired poet, with distinct touches of this strong piece of thinking flesh and blood. And Manet indicates, I think, that glimpse of the soul which one needs in a perfect likeness.

In the one done in 1865, the pride of youth, the dandy, the vivid profile, have disappeared. Here, as if in an eternal aspect, Baudelaire is shown. There is his tragic mask ; the glory of the eyes, that seem to defy life, to defy death, seems enormous, almost monstrous. The lips are closed tightly together, in their long, sinuous line, almost as if Leonardo da Vinci had stamped them with his immortality. The genius of Manet has shown the genius of Baudelaire in a gigantic shadow ; the whole face surging out of that dark shadow ; and the soul is there !

In the portrait by Carjat, his face and his eyes are contorted as if in a terrible rage ; the whole face seems drawn upward and downward in a kind of convulsion ; and the aspect, one confesses, shows a degraded type, as if all the vices he had never committed looked out of his eyes in a wild revolt.

It is in the mask of Baudelaire done by Zachari Astruc that I find almost the ethereal beauty, the sensitive nerves, the drawn lines, of the death-mask of Keats ; only, more tragic. It looks out on one as a carved image, perfect in outline, implacable, restless, sensual ; and, in that agonized face, what imagination, what enormous vitality, what strange subtlety, what devouring energy ! It might be the face of a Roman Emperor, refined, century by century, from the ghastly face of Nero, the dissolute face of Caligula, to this most modern of poets.

The Mayflower Press, Plymouth, England.
William Brendon & Son, Ltd.